CAMBRIDGE LIBRARY COLLECTION

Books of enduring scholarly value

History

The books reissued in this series include accounts of historical events and movements by eye-witnesses and contemporaries, as well as landmark studies that assembled significant source materials or developed new historiographical methods. The series includes work in social, political and military history on a wide range of periods and regions, giving modern scholars ready access to influential publications of the past.

A Handy Book for Guardians of the Poor

George C. T. Bartley KCB (1842–1910) spent twenty years as a civil servant, becoming Assistant Director in the Art and Science Department, before standing for election as a Conservative MP. He was elected in 1885 as the Member for Islington. He was a Justice of the Peace for Middlesex and Westminster, and also founded the National Penny Bank. Bartley had a keen interest in social issues, particularly poverty and education, and he wrote several books on these subjects, as well as numerous penny pamphlets aimed at improving the lives of the working class. Published in 1876, this book was based on Bartley's experiences as a Guardian of the Poor – an administrator for the Poor Law of 1834. It was written as a practical guide for anyone wishing to become involved in administering poor relief under the terms of the Poor Law.

Cambridge University Press has long been a pioneer in the reissuing of out-of-print titles from its own backlist, producing digital reprints of books that are still sought after by scholars and students but could not be reprinted economically using traditional technology. The Cambridge Library Collection extends this activity to a wider range of books which are still of importance to researchers and professionals, either for the source material they contain, or as landmarks in the history of their academic discipline.

Drawing from the world-renowned collections in the Cambridge University Library, and guided by the advice of experts in each subject area, Cambridge University Press is using state-of-the-art scanning machines in its own Printing House to capture the content of each book selected for inclusion. The files are processed to give a consistently clear, crisp image, and the books finished to the high quality standard for which the Press is recognised around the world. The latest print-on-demand technology ensures that the books will remain available indefinitely, and that orders for single or multiple copies can quickly be supplied.

The Cambridge Library Collection will bring back to life books of enduring scholarly value (including out-of-copyright works originally issued by other publishers) across a wide range of disciplines in the humanities and social sciences and in science and technology.

A Handy Book for
Guardians of the Poor

George C.T. Bartley

CAMBRIDGE
UNIVERSITY PRESS

CAMBRIDGE UNIVERSITY PRESS

Cambridge, New York, Melbourne, Madrid, Cape Town,
Singapore, São Paolo, Delhi, Tokyo, Mexico City

Published in the United States of America by Cambridge University Press, New York

www.cambridge.org
Information on this title: www.cambridge.org/9781108036856

© in this compilation Cambridge University Press 2011

This edition first published 1876
This digitally printed version 2011

ISBN 978-1-108-03685-6 Paperback

A HANDY BOOK

FOR

GUARDIANS OF THE POOR.

BEING A

COMPLETE MANUAL OF THE DUTIES OF THE OFFICE,
THE TREATMENT OF TYPICAL CASES, WITH
PRACTICAL EXAMPLES, ETC. ETC.

BY

GEORGE C. T. BARTLEY,

AUTHOR OF

"THE PARISH NET: HOW IT'S DRAGGED, AND WHAT IT CATCHES,"
"ONE SQUARE MILE IN THE EAST OF LONDON,"
"THE SEVEN AGES OF A VILLAGE PAUPER,"
ETC. ETC.

LONDON:

CHAPMAN AND HALL, 193, PICCADILLY.

1876.

PRINTED BY TAYLOR AND CO.,
LITTLE QUEEN STREET, LINCOLN'S INN FIELDS.

PREFACE.

HE object of a handbook should be evident on the face of it, and the following pages will, I hope, require but little explanation or introduction. The main object I have had before me has been to endeavour to embody in a practical form, and to arrange for practical purposes, the leading principles on which the Poor Law may be administered to the greatest advantage both to the community at large and to the individual pauper himself. In dealing with these subjects I have often heard it remarked that Reformers content themselves with general theoretic statements,—sound, no doubt, on paper, but which fail when actually brought face to face with suffering and frail humanity. This error I hope I have avoided, for I venture to assert that every treatment I suggest can and may be carried out with permanent benefit to all. I endeavour to show this not only from my practical experiences as a Guardian of the Poor, but from having for many years made the poor at their homes and in their habits my especial study.

It is considered by some that, inasmuch as the number of paupers has been on the decrease during the last few years, no steps are necessary towards reforming the administration of Relief. Such an idea appears to me to be a mistake. The prosperity of the country, the abundance of work, and the partially improved management of the poor, especially in London, having led to a reduction of the pauper roll, would seem to show that this is an especial opportunity for introducing careful reforms. In times of great national misfortune, during any continuous and general depression in trade, or during successive severe winters, it is very difficult, if not practically impossible, to make changes, however good they may theoretically be, and whatever benefits they may ultimately ensure. Starving families must be relieved; those who are in destitution must be cared for from whatever acts of folly that destitution may have arisen; but the wise legislator should in years of prosperity introduce those changes, and make those improvements, which will tend to prevent as many as possible when similar circumstances or misfortunes occur, from getting into the same evil case.

I trust that these pages may induce some at least to think seriously of becoming Guardians of the Poor who now would almost do anything rather than take on themselves this office. I do not say that there are not many excellent persons at present occupying seats on these Boards; but taking the average Poor Law Guardian, I think every one must acknowledge that a large number do not represent the education, culture, and refinement of the district to which they belong. The more I study the subject, the more convinced I am that the administration of the Poor Law is one of those social duties which should call for men of the highest attainments, and that to carry it out as it should be carried out the very best persons of leisure should be elected for the office.

GEORGE C. T. BARTLEY.

EALING, *February*, 1876.

CONTENTS.

PART I.

GENERAL.

CHAPTER I.

THE ELECTION.

 " OU should get on to the Board of Guardians," a friend once said to me. " You will thus gain a deal of information with reference to the poor in which you are interested' and, although it is a thankless task, you should certainly go through the training for a time." The truth of my friend's advice was obvious. The subject of pauperism had been my study for years, and without serving on a Board of Guardians I felt that I could not gain the practical experience which it was most desirable to possess. The same advice I venture to give to all persons of education who have any time at their disposal—for who has not, or should not have, some interest in the poor ? In the following pages I shall hope to afford to those who take my advice, as I did that of my friend, some information as

B

to their duties, and some guidance in dealing with the numerous and puzzling cases which will come before them.

I shall suppose throughout that I have before me some energetic person who has made up his mind to be a Guardian of the poor; and, judging from my own experiences, I shall bring forward those points which I myself should have been glad to have been prepared for, and I shall endeavour to illustrate each case with a few instances which have come under my own observation.

The first step which the new candidate must take is to watch for the appearance of a notice which will be put up at all the church and chapel doors in March in each year. This will announce the arrangements for the coming election for the office of Guardians of the Poor. To me, however, this lucid statement was anything but plain when I first read it with the interest of a future candidate, and I ventured to write to the Returning Officer to ask whether I was correct in the way I understood certain points. Here I went wrong, and let me warn the candidate against falling into my mistake. A request of this sort was improper, and evidently not authorised by Act of Parliament, for the Returning Officer replied, with the greatest possible politeness, that considering his official position he would not be justified in giving advice to any candidate. I innocently thought that information to a candidate was hardly advice, and could not be objected to as being contrary to any Act, and it even struck me that one of the purposes for which a Returning Officer was appointed was to ensure that the election and the candidates went right. However, I was evidently mistaken,

and, in order that my reader may not be in doubt as I was,
I will describe somewhat minutely the details of the
election.

When the notice appears on the church doors, the first
practical step in order to become a Guardian is to obtain
the proper form of nomination. This the Returning
Officer, whose name and address is on the notice
on the church door, is bound to supply on application, so that without fear he may be asked for a copy.
This form must be filled in as directed, and signed by at
least one ratepayer, and then sent back to the Returning
Officer at once, or, at any rate, before the day referred
to in the notice on the church door. When this is done,
the new candidate has complied with all that is absolutely
necessary in order to be legally a candidate, and, as far
as the law requires, nothing more has to be done.

No sooner, however, will it become known that a new
man has put up as a Guardian, particularly if he be of
some position in the district, than he will meet with his
first unpleasantness. In all probability his appearance on
the scene as a candidate will in no small degree annoy
some of his neighbours, who rather prefer to leave things
as they are, or who are interested in the existing Guardians.
This, however, he cannot help. He must thus rudely
break into the sanctity of the privileged few who have
so long had everything their own way in Parish matters.
No doubt they will oppose him, and consequently he may
find himself (as I did) let in for a contested election.
If by any accident one of the former Guardians retires and
the others do not oppose him, he will get in without even
the form of an election. This good luck, however, he can

hardly expect, and he will almost to a certainty have to go through the ordeal of a contest.

This election is conducted in the following way. On a certain day, about the first week in April (Easter Monday, of all days in the year, happened to be fixed upon the first time I was a candidate), a paper is left by a policeman at each voter's house, with the names of all the candidates printed on it. This document sets forth the numerous penalties for false returns, alarming clauses showing how votes may be informally given and the consequences thereof, but scarcely enough information—for a constituency, perhaps somewhat dull in grasping printed details,—as to how the form should be properly filled up. The main thing, however, is for the voter to indicate for whom he or she wishes to vote by scratching out the other names. Two days afterwards, or in some places one day, the policeman returns for this valuable polling-paper, which in the meantime is supposed to have been duly filled up. He is not bound to wait for it when he comes, and he has a long round to take during the day ; all, therefore, who are anxious about voting should almost waylay the collecting policeman lest he should disappear before they can give him the paper, and their rightful privilege of a British elector be thus lost.

The new candidate will do well to draw up a short circular explaining his notions and claim for acting on the Board of Guardians, and also clearly and familiarly describing, without threats of pains and penalties, how the voting paper may be filled up so as to secure his return. This circular he should distribute to all or as many of the residents in the parish to which he belongs as he possibly can about two days before the voting-papers are sent out. He must remember that every ratepayer has a vote, and though large ratepayers have two votes or even more up to a maximum of six, yet it is the small people as a rule who decide the election. He need not be particular therefore in selecting houses at which to leave his address, but he should do so at every house and cottage in the district. When I went through this operation I left a large number myself, and a great deal of information I thus obtained.

" Have you had one of my papers," I said to one who I hoped would soon be among my constituents. He was a large employer of labour of a peculiar description. During the spring and summer he required a great many hands, but in the winter very few. All he employed were of the poorest class, and the majority of them women and children.

" They tell me, sir, that you want to get rid of out-door relief."

" Well, yes, certainly I should like to do so gradually," I replied, " but not immediately."

" Then I can't vote for you, that's clear."

" I am sorry for that," I replied, " the great object I have in view is to reduce the number of poor, and I think that the present system of wholesale out-door relief not only demoralizes but actually increases poverty and suffering."

" There must be great good in it though all the same," he replied, " and I should object to getting rid of it ; that would never do. So good morning, sir ; I am sorry I can't vote for you."

Now, not to be uncharitable, this case was typical of a great many others. Probably nine out of every ten of the persons employed by this individual received out-door relief, certainly during the winter. Many were widows with families, others were broken down men and such-like, who were able to do the work required, for most of it was not very heavy though tiring and continuous. They were paid very low wages and were taken on for a week or two at a time as required, and then got rid of, when they at once returned to the Parish allowance, and indeed many probably never lost it. Any stricter system of out-door relief would involve their being struck off the Parish List at once, and this would mean a considerable increase to the weekly wage list of their employer, from the necessity of their continuous employment in order to secure them when wanted.

Another of my constituents was more hopeful. He was gardening, so I gave him the circular and told him what it was.

" Are you the gentleman himself ? " said he.

" Yes, I am, and shall be glad to answer as many questions as you like to ask," I replied.

" Well, all I can say is we want some fresh blood on the Board. I know of no end of cases getting regular out-door relief who have no more right to it than you or I. The whole thing wants going into, and so I shall vote for you if it's only to get some fresh man on the Board."

" I am much obliged to you. I quite agree that the whole thing wants going into, and I believe not only in the interests of the ratepayers but much more so for the benefit of the poor themselves."

Another voter was very glad to see me, and would vote

or me, because a short time before he had heard a lecture from me which he said had interested him much.

The tradesmen of the village must be secured by the new candidate if possible. They have great influence. I received a most amusing letter from one thanking me for being so kind as to offer myself as a candidate. His only fear was whether I could devote the necessary time to the work, for he evidently had some proper notion of the importance of the duties even of a Guardian of the Poor.

The interest of the clergy and ministers of the district should also by all means if possible be elicited in the new candidate's favour. The clergy and ministers have much power, and according to their action a great deal of substantial help may be given or withheld. Even, however, if the new Guardian cannot secure this support, he need not be alarmed at the prospects of his success, for he may take comfort from the thought that those who will vote for any one who is new are numerous. He must distribute his circulars freely, and take a little trouble in seeing as many people as he can, and talking rather pleasantly with them ; and if he does this he will probably be successful, even though he find himself, as I did, at the bottom of the list of elected candidates.

CHAPTER II.

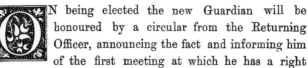N being elected the new Guardian will be
honoured by a circular from the Returning
Officer, announcing the fact and informing him
of the first meeting at which he has a right
to attend the Board of Guardians. If he is unsuccessful
he will receive no notice, and silence in this case will mean
failure. The first meeting will be about the third week in
April, and the hour depends of course on the habits of
the particular Board to which he belongs ; but generally it is
at 11 o'clock. At this first meeting, as a rule, the Board is
pretty well represented except by the ex-officio Guardians,
who rarely attend. The table in the Board-room in the larger
Unions is usually in the shape of a printed U, the members
sitting round the outside of it, and the space up the
middle being reserved for the unfortunate creatures who
present themselves for relief. By this arrangement every
member may have a good look at the applicant, who is
at it were obliged to run the gauntlet before the whole
assembly. Some Unions have but a spacious table of

ordinary construction, and in a large and scattered district the applicant is not as a rule required to be present.

The first duty of the first meeting is for the clerk to read a statement concerning the recent election, and the new Guardian will have the satisfaction of knowing his place on the poll. The next duty is to elect the Chairman and Vice-chairman, and usually, after the delivery of the customary flattering speeches all round, the gentlemen who acted in this capacity the former year are re-elected unanimously. The reappointment of the standing committees comes next. These are the House and School Visiting Committees, the Finance Committee, and the Assessment Committee. If the new Guardian have plenty of time at his disposal, he should be on all these; but, if not, the first is the most important as regards the details of the Poor Law administration itself.

Next will come the ordinary routine work of the Board, namely, the consideration of the applicants for relief. The number of these of course varies with the Union and the season of the year. In my own Union we had on an average about 100 adults and 100 children; but this is a large number. In many Unions each case is simply described in the Chairman's book, with a few particulars of age, occupation, whether married or single, and the number of children. Sometimes lists of each week's applicants with the above particulars are prepared by the children of the school, so that each Guardian may have the cases with this information about them before him. Whatever other and further details are needed have to be extracted, if possible, from the relieving officers, who are all present for that purpose. Each officer explains shortly the cases

from his district, and usually recommends the action to
be taken on them. The rate at which in some large
Unions the applicants are despatched will surprise the new
Guardian, as it did me at my first meetings. I calculated
that the average time per case, often involving relief to half-
a-dozen people or more, was less than forty-five seconds.

It was a little strange, and perhaps somewhat demoralis-
ing that at the very first meeting of the Board, at which I
was present, a direct breach of the law was knowingly
and intentionally committed. The following were the
circumstances. A child whose history a member of the
Board had evidently gone into carefully, had a chance of
being apprenticed to a respectable man, who stated that
as an act of charity he was willing to remit £10 of the
usual apprenticing fee, namely £25. The Guardian and
some friends had got together £10, and the Board was
asked to pay £5 to complete the sum necessary. If this
were done, the boy would be taken off the Parish for some
years, he would be taught a trade, and, it was argued with
some truth, might be made a respectable citizen, for the
employer would have to keep him in his own house all the
time of his apprenticeship. If every pauper in the
country could be disposed of at this rate, or at ten times
this rate, no doubt it would be a cheap bargain. The
Board quite saw the point and was willing to agree to it,
but was it legal? The clerk was applied to, and stated
that such an expenditure was not legal *unless it was put
down as an outfit!* This was a loophole, and the money
was voted, and as an outfit was this £5 put down in the
accounts, though I need hardly say it was no more an
outfit than a champagne dinner would have been.

Sometimes the most peculiar applications are made on these occasions by paupers and others. Once I remember a single woman of 25 years of age requested to be informed whether her child of 2½ years old was " too young to swear." The woman was likely again to become a mother, and the swearing applied to the child giving evidence against the reputed father. The Board naturally declined to give any opinion.

When the out-door applicants are settled off, it is usual for the Master of the Workhouse to make a report. He announces those who wish to go away from the workhouse, and they generally appear before the Board, hoping to get "a trifle to leave the house." If they have behaved well this request is granted, and a shilling or two and some loaves, according to the family, are given to them. Not unfrequently the Master has to report a refractory inmate, when the culprit is sent for and reprimanded.

"This woman, sir, is about the worst tempered woman we have ever had in the house," I once heard the Master report of an inmate who was standing before the Board, and her looks certainly bore out the statement. It appeared she helped in the kitchen, and if any one even touched her dress accidentally in passing she would threaten to throw the boiling water at them, and was generally so alarming that no one knew what to do with her. She was cautioned and retired somewhat humbled. Extreme cases of indolence and refusing to work are also brought up, and the culprits either look determinately dogged or stutter out excuses. One day a wretched-looking creature, I remember, who strongly objected to the work of sawing ends of timber for firewood, urged as an excuse that he could not saw it straight. I need hardly say he was simply told to saw it crooked.

Miscellaneous applications also come from the Master of the Workhouse at these times. If he wants stores, repairs, or anything of the sort, the House Committee recommend the purchase, and it is ordered by the Board on their report. A very curious detail I shall not easily forget shows that fashion and a sense of the correct thing is not unknown even among the inmates of the Workhouse. Perhaps on no point are they so particular as in all matters relating to funerals, and although it be but a pauper funeral, it should, they consider, be done properly. The offending cause on this occasion was the coat of the Union hearse driver, and the Master of the House applied for a new one. It appeared that it was notorious and had been repeatedly remarked that though "the horse looked very good, and so did the hearse, the driver's coat was *tarnation* bad." I am glad to be able to add that the scandal was put an end to by the Board ordering a new coat.

The next routine is for the Board-room to be cleared, with the exception of the Guardians, the Clerks, and the Reporters, that is, when the last are allowed to be present at all. The Minutes of the last meeting are then read, and any special business is gone into. If any letter has been received from the Local Government Board, it is read; if any member of the Board has a motion to bring forward or any complaint to make, it is then considered and discussed. After this the Board breaks up.

The various Committees meet usually at 10 o'clock on Board-days. The Finance Committee has, of course, a good deal of detail to attend to, as has also the House Committee. The Assessment Committee's duties are not so numerous on ordinary occasions, though they often produce great discontent and serious complaints throughout the Union by those who consider themselves aggrieved in the assessments of their own property.

In some of the largest Unions the applicants for relief are not considered by the whole Board but by Committees of the Board. When this is done the Board is split up and a certain number attend each week, and the whole body only assembles once a month. This is by far the best plan, for it is obvious that if the regulations on which relief shall be given are broadly determined, it is a waste of power to have some thirty persons considering each case.

The exact mode of procedure in each Union of course varies, and the new Guardian will soon find out the specialities of his own district. I have, therefore, merely generally sketched out the main points, and will now proceed to consider the various characteristic cases of pauperism and relief which will, I fear, be found to be but too common in all Unions.

PART II.

SPECIAL EVILS CONSEQUENT ON RELIEF
AND THEIR TREATMENT.

CHAPTER III.

THE HABIT OF DEPENDENCE ON THE PARISH AND ITS
TREATMENT.

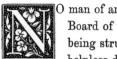O man of any intelligence can possibly sit at a
Board of Guardians for many weeks without
being struck with the system of hopeless and
helpless dependence which the present Poor
Law has succeeded in establishing among a section of the
community. The cases that will come before him will be
endless. He will see able and hearty persons on the least
difficulty or trouble come to the Parish as a matter of
course; he will hear them ask for everything they want,
clothes, boots, shoes, surgical and other instruments even
though costing but a few shillings, medical aid, etc. etc.
In fact by the number and variety of the applications he

may be led to think the Parish is a tender parent of a very large family.

No phase of our pauperism is more unsatisfactory than this. Dependence is of all characteristics in a people the least desirable, and a nation composed of those who cannot and will not look to their own energies in case of trouble, can never rank high. Englishmen as a rule are proverbial for their independence, courage, and reliance on themselves, and if anything tends more than another to condmen the present administration of the Poor Law it is the fact that so many thousands, in spite of our natural characteristic, are kept chronically in this state of abject dependence on the dole of relief.

To illustrate this habit of dependence I will give a few typical cases out of hundreds which have come before me. On one occasion in the height of summer an able-bodied man of 58, with no children and in full work, asked the Parish, as a matter of course, to take care of his sick wife in a cheap way. He said he would pay something, but he wanted her to be sent to the Workhouse because that was cheap.

I have seen on another occasion a woman appeal to the Parish to take her husband, as he was too much trouble at home, and feel quite injured if the Guardians did not at once do what she asked. Another instance I may mention was that of a respectable man with six children. He brought his eldest daughter to a Board and asked the Guardians to take her in, as she suffered from St. Vitus's dance.

The poor girl was evidently afflicted, but inasmuch as the man owned himself to be earning 30/- a week regularly, besides what his wife and children brought in, the Guardians wisely in this case did not allow the ratepayers to be burdened with the cost of his child.

I once heard a somewhat amusing case of a woman who on behalf of her daughter applied for an outfit of clothes. It appeared that the daughter had just got a situation as a domestic servant, and that was made the excuse for the appeal. The Board refused to give the clothes, on which the woman got most abusive, stormed at the Guardians, and wound up with saying,

" You ought to be much obliged to me for having got married again, for I've saved you the money you used to give me when I lost my first husband. All I can say is I 'ope you'll all want clothes yerselves before you die ! ! "

There was spirit at any rate here, which is a better sign than the abject dependence which is often to be witnessed.

Examples without number might be added, but I fear to be tedious, though I cannot refrain from giving the following instance which came before me. It appeared that with a couple, in tolerable circumstances, the not altogether unheard-of coincidence had happened, that the man and his wife did not get on very well together, and to make matters worse the man at the age of 49 from some cause or other had become ill. The wife was an able-bodied woman who managed to earn something considerable, though no doubt she found it troublesome to get on with the incubus of her husband. She accordingly applied to her friend the Parish, to relieve her by taking him into the Workhouse. The Board declined, and stated in reply to more than one application of the same kind that inasmuch as she was perfectly able to maintain herself and husband, the husband alone could not be taken into the house, but that if the relief of the house was given, it must be to both husband and wife. This, however, the woman did not at all approve of, and after several attempts to bring the Parish to reason, she wrote the following letter to the relieving officer who handed it to the Board :

"Mr. Ashford i cannot suport my husband i find it unposobel thearfore i have left him i have don my duty by him as a wife hoping the Parish will do thears from me.
"E. Browne."

Suiting the action to the word she departed, and the Parish had of course after this to take in the man.

Sometimes a refusal to do what is wanted leads to threats and intimidation on the part of the would-be paupers, which are not carried out quite so decidedly as in the last case. I made a note of an Irish woman who one day came before a Board and literally demanded aid towards the cost of going to America with her children. She was told the Parish could not aid in emigration or help her in the way she wished, "Then you'll take the consequences," she replied, "for I'll lave me children behind me." As she went out of the room, she turned round and cried out in a defiant manner again, "I'll pledge ye me word that I'll lave the children behind me." I am glad to add, however, that she preferred to break her word to carrying out her threat. No doubt she really had ample means of taking her children with her, and only wanted to get what she could in addition from the Parish.

C

Nothing perhaps is a greater agent for promoting dependence than the medical out-door relief as now administered, and concerning which I dwell more fully in another chapter. This relief is looked upon altogether as a matter of course, and the receiver does not consider him or herself as a pauper in consequence of receiving it. I remember an old woman of 63 coming for an allowance for herself and husband. It was stated for her that she had never been on the Parish before, and I accordingly asked her if this was so. She at once said yes, she had never been here before except " of course " when her husband had been ill.

A feature which will strike a new Guardian with much concern is that not a few cases will convince him, though unwillingly, that this spirit of dependence is spreading upwards in society and is not confined to the very poor. Some indeed of the very poor are noble examples of independence in spite of most cruel hardships, but I have seen some instances which show that fairly well-to-do persons are not above the Parish relief if they can get it for themselves or their family, and are even not ashamed to ask for it.

As an example of this I may mention the following circumstances. A man who until quite lately had been in a good position, and who had been living in a house rated at £40 a year, disappeared and left behind him three small children. The mother also seemed to be dead or to have disappeared. The man's brother and his wife accordingly presented themselves before the Board of Guardians. They were evidently well-to-do people, even more so than their brother had been. They stated that they had several children of their own, but they altogether refused to support or to help to support their nephews and nieces, and by law they were not bound to do so. When asked who was keeping them at the moment, the man replied that they were in his house, though he could not give them anything and they were starving. The Parish had to remove the unfortunate children to the Workhouse and to take proceedings against the father if he could be caught. No doubt, it would have been hard upon the brother to keep the children, but many a labouring man with less than a pound a week has done it over and over again ; and the fact of a man in this position throwing his nephews and nieces on the Parish is of itself very suggestive of the extension of the spirit of dependence.

One more case of a similar kind I will give, and that is one of a man engaged permanently at very superior work, and who would probably have felt somewhat injured at being even called an artisan. He owned to be earning regularly £2. 10s. a week and more by extra work, but he had the misfortune to be burdened with an afflicted wife. It appeared that somehow or other (through some charity) he had got her off his hands for a time, but she had been returned to him, and he accordingly applied to have her kept in the Workhouse. The chairman informed him that his request was not creditable ; that he should send her to some institution, for he was decidedly able to pay the expense. The man replied that they would not take her in under from £4 to £6 a year, and so he thought the Parish ought to keep her. In other words, though he was earning 50s. a week at least, he thought it hard to pay 2s. a week towards the maintenance of his afflicted wife.

The judicious treatment of cases of dependence may well be thought a difficulty by any Guardian, and especially by a new one. Of course, after a long life of reliance on the Parish, cure is next door to impossible. The injudicious relief has been in no small degree the cause of the dependence and it would be cruel to visit all the consequences on the pauper by any sudden change or refusal of relief. At the same time, however, much may be done by care and patience. For the young who, owing to some misfortune, are beginning a life of dependence, relief by loan* for the first or perhaps the second application will be found the most salutary means of arresting the disease. In not a few cases a spirit of independence will be inculcated by the enforcement of the weekly repayments. Others who may not be thus improved, will soon see that as they have to repay the amount granted to them when they are well, they may as well try to do without the aid of the Parish altogether, and not be troubled by the relieving officer. I would strongly recommend that whenever this spirit of dependence is shown, if out-door relief is given at all, it should be on loan, the repayment of which must be rigidly enforced, and that this rule shall be universally adopted with all persons under 40 years of age. On a second or at most a third application for relief from the same person, even if for medical aid, unless the applicant belong to some medical club or provident dispensary, out-door relief should be refused altogether. The Workhouse must in these cases be offered, unless there are some really very special circumstances, and the persons can give some evidence of having in the meantime done something to

* See chapter 30—On Loans.

indicate that he or she has learned to some extent at least to depend on him or herself. Hard as this rule may be thought, and painful though it may be to administer even with care and caution, it will be found in a year or two vastly to reduce the sufferings now caused by this sad habit of dependence on the Parish, and which the dole is quite powerless to avert.

CHAPTER IV.

THE HABIT OF INDOLENCE AND ITS TREATMENT.

OLLOWING the importance of independence and self-reliance, and almost, indeed, an essential element in these qualities, comes industry. Without industry any nation must soon fall, and Englishmen as they are independent and boast of it, so may they pride themselves on being industrious and hardworking. The Poor Law and its results may therefore be judged not unreasonably by its effect on industry with that class of the community with whom it deals, and here the new Guardian of the poor will find enough serious matter to occupy his attention, though the cause and effect of injudicious relief as it affects industry will not always be apparent at first sight.

One common peculiarity which will strike the inexperienced member of the Board will be the unanimous answer that he will hear as to the impossibility of getting work. He may himself have a number of barges standing idle within a few yards of the Board-room for want of the very labour which the applicant professes, and which he cannot get supplied at any price, and yet he will hear this excuse of "no work" urged to his very face. Strange as this may seem, it is not altogether unnatural, and the Board of Guardians themselves unknowingly encourage it but too often. In fact the system itself may be said to be responsible for it, for with the careless investigation of the circumstances of each case which is so common (chapter 28), an indolent fellow really fares better than an industrious one, his loss of wages during his time of indolence being made up by the Parish money. With children the evil of this system is immense; and I must give an example which is typical, exactly as it came under my own observation. A widow who had several children, the eldest child being a boy of twelve, presented herself before a Board of Guardians. She was a respectable-looking woman who had received relief since her widowhood, and she applied for its renewal; she was asked why her eldest boy did not earn something, and she said he could not, and although the relieving officer informed the Board that the very boy had been engaged in distributing newspapers before going to school in the morning, and that he had been taken off from the work simply because he had had a headache the week before, yet liberal out-door relief was continued to the widow, and this very child was taken into account as one of the family in computing that relief. I made further inquiries into this case, and I found that the newspaper shop was kept by a hard-working widow, who paid rates and taxes. She was in constant trouble about getting boys to distribute her papers. The headache referred to in this particular case was nothing at all, the boy had a long time been most troublesome and inattentive. She paid the boys two-and-sixpence, and even three-and-sixpence a week for an hour's work or so in the morning before they went to school. She had tried almost every boy in the village, but they only stayed a week or two, though numbers of widows with children were receiving Parish money, and asserting weekly at the Board of Guardians that they could scarcely live. At last this unfortunate newsagent had to give up the newspaper trade altogether, though it was a large part of her living.

Not unfrequently I have noticed that the unguarded remarks of the Guardians must have a most discouraging effect on industry. On one occasion I saw an old woman of 61 come to the Board; she said she hoped to go hop-picking in a fortnight or so; one-and-sixpence and a loaf a week was given her for four weeks on the understanding that if she "went hopping it would not be continued." No doubt she took the hint and did not go.

Another common mode of encouraging indolence may be gathered from the following example. A widow of but twenty-eight years, able-bodied, with four children came before a Board. "You used to earn something, don't you do that now?" said the chairman. "No, sir, I don't earn anything now." Out-door relief was accordingly given without another word. No doubt the inference of cause and effect was not intended by the chairman, but a sharp young woman would not fail to notice it, to draw her own conclusions, and to repeat the same to her circle of acquaintances.

To discourage indolence in widows is not easy, for it is difficult to act wisely without regard to senti-ment or the remarks which may be made by superficial observers. The problem (chapter 9) is how to steer clear of harshness and at the same time not to pauperise and promote indolent habits. Relief being usually given so readily to widows, and the very fact of this sad condition being, in many Unions, almost *per se* sufficient to secure Parish relief, it is not to be wondered at that habits of industry are but too often seriously discouraged. I have known many cases where relief has been granted and continued for years almost without a word of inquiry, where even the relief granted to a widow with children has remained the same, though the children have grown up and even left the neighbourhood. This is negligent relief; but even the granting relief as a matter of course in early widowhood, thus announcing that relief is an acknowledged certainty under such circumstances, is a most serious mistake. It throws as it were a wet blanket on industry, to say nothing of its effect on the thrift of all the young couples in the neighbourhood, who might, if they only thought about it, be providing something for themselves in case of a rainy day overtaking them. Even to a hard-working and superior woman the notion that she has but to ask in order to secure the Parish money is sufficient, as indeed experience proves, to prevent many from at once relying on their own efforts.

I remember a case coming before me which is just in point. It was that of a widow about thirty-five years of age; she had a pleasant face, but evidently somewhat of a temper. Her husband had died suddenly a few months before, leaving her with seven children, but he had been so much respected that the neighbours had collected some forty pounds for her. This money was paying her rent, her sister was making a pound a week as a washerwoman according to the widow's own account, and they worked together. The widow earned, she said, ten shillings a week, though there was no satisfactory explanation why she made so much less out of the business than her sister. One or two of the elder children must have been helping her materially. Her dress was really remarkably good, including black kid gloves, and her general appearance was in every respect superior. She had had relief since her widowhood, and had already learned to grumble at the Parish bread which was not good enough. She succeeded, however, in getting money and bread, and a year after I found she was still a pauper. This woman but for the Poor Law would undoubtedly have earned her living independently, and been a respectable member of society. As it was, the habit of coming repeatedly to beg, the habit she was getting into of making the worst of things, the premium she found to be set on earning little, and so forth, were tending rapidly to make the woman a confirmed and indolent pauper.

As regards the treatment of these cases, I will venture to say for the guidance of new Guardians that indications of a loss or diminution of industry following out-door relief should be carefully watched and most rigorously stopped. Less hardships by far will ensue by offering only the Workhouse than by allowing this habit to be formed. If this step be taken at once the " house " will not be accepted, but the threat and withdrawal of out-door relief will bring back the habit of industry and self-reliance. With able-bodied men, however large their families, the house alone should be given as, indeed, the law provides ;

with women without children also it will be found in the long-run far more humane to refuse out-door relief than to undermine their habits of industry. Even to widows with families out-door relief must not be granted as a matter of course, and unless there be special considerations, as referred to in another chapter (chapter 9), relief must on no account in any case be permanent, nor must it be reckoned upon and made to take the place of honest industry. Directly this is found to be commencing, either by the person professing (without any sufficient reason) to be earning less, or if it is evident that the parents or the children do not make every effort and avail themselves of every means of labour, the out-door relief must be at once firmly cut off. This may seem hard, but it is the true kindness, for be it remembered not only is the person, him or herself, to be considered, but the fate of a whole family of children is at stake. That is to say, the present action of the Guardians will determine whether these little ones are to grow into industrious and independent members of society or to swell the band of hereditary paupers.

CHAPTER V.

HE discouragement to thrift is perhaps one of the most obvious evils of the present Poor Law System, and no new Guardian of the Poor can fail to be struck with this fact if he attends at all to his duty. Instances without number will come before him, and he will not only see that thrift is indirectly and even directly discouraged, but he will be led to think that the reverse habit, namely, absolute improvidence is indeed promoted.

Take for instance a very common case. A man who has been engaged for years on a railway, or in some large institution at good wages, having a wife and two or three children, is taken ill. He is knocked off work, and immediately applies to the Parish, perhaps the very next day, for out-door relief. Most Boards give it him at once, and I think I may say that in my own Union and within my own experience elsewhere, I have never seen any other action taken in such a case. If it be asked whether there is any club at the railway, the relieving-officer will say there is, but that this man would not join it. His wife if she is present will remark that, "her husband never did hold to clubs." Of course not, the Parish is a better one ; she belongs to that, and he can draw out of it on all occasions when he thus requires it without having to pay anything in. Can any one wonder at so many of such cases not belonging to the club? I certainly do not, the marvel to me is that any of the poor join these clubs. It shows what an independent spirit there is in spite of the action of the Poor Law.

These cases, in which it "does not suit persons" to belong to clubs by which they might by their own efforts avoid coming on to the rates are common, and cannot fail to be suggestive to an inexperienced Guardian. I once heard a woman openly state it without the least hesitation. She had four children, and her husband had been taken ill a few days before she applied to the Parish; out-door relief was at once given her, and in reply to a question as to why her husband had not belonged to a club, she stated that "it did not suit him to do so."

Unwise to say the least of it as this action is, for in all such cases out-door relief should be absolutely refused, it is strictly within the spirit of the existing Poor Law. By the strict letter of that law, no out-door relief may be given to a member of a club, for the simple reason that he is not destitute. The absurdity of this law is so obvious that it is repeatedly broken ; in fact, very few if any out-door paupers are really destitute. It is fortunate indeed for them that they are not so ; for if they were, starvation alone would be their lot with the pittances they receive, which are in very few cases sufficient to keep body and soul together.

Sometimes slight efforts are made to encourage thrift, in spite of the above law, as may be judged from the following case. A man, near London, with four children, who when in work earned but 18*s.* a week, managed also to belong to a good club. He was taken ill and his wife applied to the Parish. She of course said nothing about his thrift, fearing no doubt that it would as usual go against her. A Guardian, however, asked her and brought out the fact that he was getting 10*s.* a week from the club. As a sort of set-off or palliation she stated that the week before she had had to pay 2*s.* 6*d.* and this week 2*s.* for leeches alone; 4*s.* and six loaves were given her, an amount as she was informed *very little less*, owing to the Board's desire to promote thrift, than would have been granted her had her husband not belonged to a club.

Evident as it must be how discouraging such a system is to the poor, who at best can save and endeavour to be independent under great difficulties, the worst cases are those of persons who strive all their lives and do not find out the consequences until too late. They avoid all connection with the Parish while they can work ; they do not consider it concerns them to learn its system. They hold themselves above it ; they try to put by if it be only a little, hanging on to the fond hope that if the worst come to the worst in their old age, they may be able to get a little aid from the Parish to add to their own savings. Poor deluded creatures ! They see all their neighbours, however bad and worthless, ending their days with the Parish dole, but having kept out of the Parish atmosphere, they have not learned the plan by which alone such advantages can be secured.

Let me give one or two examples from many which have come before my own experience. An old man presented himself at a board at which I was present. He had been for very many years, all his working life indeed, in the service of a nobleman, the owner of large estates in the Union, as a farm-labourer. So good had been his conduct that he had received a pension of 7s. a week. This money at last when other little savings had gone, was not enough to keep himself and his wife, as they required somewhat extra nourishment now they were very old. In this difficulty he appealed to the Board ; a discussion took place. Was he destitute ? Ought not the nobleman to keep him ? etc. All out-door relief was refused, and he was merely offered the house for himself and wife, when of course, as it was stated, the pension would come to the Parish towards the keep of the old couple. Had he never got a pension, he would have been given out-door relief at once like hundreds of others. Had he behaved so badly that he had been dismissed, he would have been treated far better by the Parish. Had he been a drunken fellow, spending everything at the Public-house, the Board would not have hesitated to give him that out-door relief which was now refused for the simple reason that he had a small pension, obviously too insignificant to enable him and his wife to live on, as they deserved to live to the end of their days.

Another case I may mention is that of a widow of 65, who I saw apply for out-door relief. She had been steady and careful all her life, her husband had got together a little shop, but since his death she had become unable to continue it. Accordingly she, some years before, had sold the shop on the understanding that she was to have £5 a year from it, or somewhat less than 2s. a week as long as she lived. Several of the Guardians protested against such a person coming to the Parish at all, and out-door relief was granted only by a narrow division. This was to consist of but a shilling and a loaf a week, though had she been on and off the rates all her life, had she not by her industry provided something for her old age (though true what she had been able to provide was not enough to keep her from starvation), much more liberal relief would have been granted at once.

At times people who try to help themselves literally fall between two stools, and they must indeed curse their own folly in trying to avoid the Parish. Consider the following case. A man with three children broke his leg. He belonged to the Odd Fellows, and for some weeks received 10s. a week. Owing to some dispute, however, the Odd Fellows would not continue the benefit as long as the rules specified, as the doctor said the man could work. The Union doctor, on the other hand, certified that he had two large open wounds still in his leg, and that he was quite unfit to stand upon it. What was he to do? His wife came to the Parish, and literally between the two stools this poor family was like to fall to the ground. Several Guardians protested against giving him relief at all, as he should make the Odd Fellows do it. In the meantime what was the family to live on? After a long discussion they were handed over to the relieving officer to relieve at his discretion, and a report was to be brought up the next week. Had they never belonged to a club at all liberal out-door relief would have been granted without a word.

The right policy for any Guardian, wishing to improve his Union, in cases of the nature referred to in this chapter is obvious. Thrift is the one if not the only antidote to pauperism, and every act of a Board of Guardians should, as far as possible, encourage this habit. True, the law in this respect is bad and most unwise, but it is so palpably wrong that it is broken and set at nought with the consent of the head authorities. On the same principle that I ventured to recommend in a previous chapter, that out-door relief should be rigidly refused in cases of improvidence, so would I urge upon every new Guardian that he should vote in all cases for the most liberal out-door relief for those who have done what they can to help themselves. I would tell them that so much was given because they belonged to this or that club, or because they had provided or tried to provide in this or that way. I would let the whole Union know of this policy, and the Union would soon reap the benefit. Why should their thrift and savings go against them in old age or misfortune ?*

* 'Thrift as the Out-Door Relief Test.' Bell and Daldy. See advertisements at end of book.

CHAPTER VI.

AMONG the many vices for the encouragement of which the Poor Law has to answer, that of deception stands out pre-eminently. In every way deception is encouraged, and the new Guardian will not fail to be struck with this sad reality. There is deception as to the earnings, as to impossibility to get work, as to the wages for that work, as to the illness of the husband, or wife, or child, as to the assistance received from friends, as to the charity elicited from patrons, as to the possibility of children helping, and in fact as to every point. The reason for all this is obvious and simple. The Poor Law gives its benefits with the greatest liberality to those who appear the worst off; destitution is made the passport to relief, and each applicant therefore tries to qualify, asserts that he is in as bad a plight as he possibly can be, and Boards of Guardians in but too many cases do not take trouble enough to investigate each case, and to sift it thoroughly. Consequently by taking the applicant's statements pretty much as they are given, in most Unions it has long been found by the paupers, who are very sharp after their own interests, that those get most who make out the worst case. The chances are a hundred to one if the deception will be discovered, for the relieving officer has not time, nor does he take the trouble, to ferret out facts which his masters do not show much anxiety to possess. If, however, by any stroke of misfortune the deception does come to light, what does it matter? There are no penalties, the relief can but then be stopped till by some clever device it is secured again, and consequently the most barefaced and even, if it be not an anomaly to say so, the most open deception is frequently practised on Boards of Guardians.

The new Guardian will be surprised at some of the statements he will hear. He will soon get accustomed to women well-dressed, plump, and comfortable looking, who will assert they exist on but one day's washing a week at 1s. 6d., and that they have no other means whatever of living; to men who will say they cannot by any means get work though he may know that labour of all kinds is in demand in the very parish from which they came. He will hear applicants stoutly assert that the paupers they represent are next to dying, though they may have been seen about, possibly at the public house, the day before. Cases without number of this sort might be given, but they lose much of their point as the individual applicants cannot be brought personally before my reader. At the very first meeting the new Guardian will probably have his credulity stretched to the utmost. The following example I cannot refrain from giving, as it shows the regular plan of deception which is sometimes laid before coming to the Parish, and the cloven foot comes out so simply that I could hardly have believed the story had I not myself been present on the occasion when it was narrated.

An old woman of 68 came to the Board where I was and asked for relief. Her husband was somewhat infirm, and so she thought, I suppose, she might as well get a little from the Parish of what was going in the general scramble. She made a good living with a pony and cart, as a hawker of vegetables and such like. Knowing, however, that the luxurious possession of a horse and cart might be objected to, in her appeal to the Parish, she put the said horse and cart into the keeping of some friend as it were in trust for her. The relieving officer had, however, been too sharp, and had found out all about her, as she was indeed known in the district as a well-to-do person.

" What do you want of us? " said the chairman to her.

" A little relief, sir, if you please. My husband is very bad, and I am not so young as I used to be."

" We hear you have a horse and cart, so you can't be destitute," replied the chairman.

"Oh! the old pony, sir. Mr. Jones has got that, now."

" Have you sold it then? "

"No, sir, not exactly, sir; but he's got it."

"Then it's still yours? "

" Well, in a sort of a way, yes sir," she replied, rather hesitatingly, feeling she had been defeated somewhat.

"Then you can't be destitute, for I suppose the horse and cart is worth something," said a member of the Board, " It's worth two pounds maybe? "

"I should be very sorry to take ten for it," replied the woman, fancying she was dealing as usual, and forgetting for a moment where she was, and the effect of such a speech.

"Just so, then we can't give you any out-door relief, but if you like to wait below for an order you can have one, and come into the Workhouse with your husband."

"That I shall never do," replied the woman, as she flounced out of the room.

The next time she comes to theParish she will be more careful no doubt, and deceive us a little more successfully.

The action in these cases of deception every one will at once say must be obvious. It should be discouraged. No doubt it should, but the amount of it which is practised makes it evident that the present mode of dealing with such fraud is not successful. The real cause of the evil is the imperfect investigation made by the relieving officer into the previous circumstances and history of the individual. (See chapter 28.) True, there are many cases where the deception is apparent on the face of them, as, for instance, person existing solely on eighteenpence a week, but more often the deception is not so open, and the real cause of its success in obtaining out-door relief, and its consequent growth, is caused by a knowledge throughout the Union of carelessness and the imperfect nature of the relieving officers' investigations. Whenever deception however is detected, out-door relief should be refused altogether, and the House alone given. Very few of this class of pauper will ever take the House; for those who deceive most, and are the greatest offenders in this respect, are generally fairly off and make a good living in a variety of ways. Whenever persons assert that they live on eighteenpence a week, or some other impossible sum, the House should certainly be offered at once, and out-door relief refused, for if their statement be correct, surely such systematic starvation should be stopped, and if it be not correct the sooner a stop is put to such deception the better.

The new Guardian need not therefore be at a loss in dealing with these cases. If he succeed in introducing a more systematic investigation, as urged in chapter 28, deception will almost die out as a natural consequence. Until however he can carry this reform, he may be quite happy in acting strictly, and declining out-door relief whenever deception is practised as a means of securing the Parish money.

CHAPTER VII.

THE HABIT OF CHILDREN NEGLECTING THEIR PARENTS, AND ITS TREATMENT.

NE of the saddest considerations in connection with Parish relief, is the encouragement which the system gives to children to neglect their parents. The law requires children to aid their parents if they can, but married daughters are exempt from all liability, and I have seen well-to-do women, keep. ing large shops and public-houses, allowing their old parents to get the Parish half-crown, and refusing all aid. "For why," say they, "should we save the rates?" Owing to the frequent neglect of a thorough investigation, cases go on for years in which parents receive an allowance from the Parish though their children may be in excellent situations and quite able to keep them. If however it ever happens that the fact is discovered, the children usually betake themselves away, and so elude the Parish. The parents are forced to encourage them in this unnatural conduct, for very peace sake. I once heard a woman account for her son's absence, and consequent neglect of aiding her, remark when asked where he was, "Oh! he's onywhere like." Of course she knew, but she would not, or dared not say.

Besides encouraging this state of things by imperfect investigation, many Boards promote it by granting out-door relief, and not taking the trouble to summon the children before a magistrate to show cause why they do not do their duty. Take, for instance, such a case as this which came before me. A widow had been receiving relief for years, and it was not known that she had children. It now appeared, however, that she had four sons, one holding an excellent berth, another with two children earning twenty-two shillings a week, another with three children earning the same, and a third in a similar position, unmarried. Instead of refusing out-door relief altogether, and at once taking steps to enforce these children to do their duty, 1s. 6d. and a loaf was continued. Not one on the Board would even second the proposal to make any change.

Again, let me mention another case. An old widow of eighty-seven was in receipt of 2s. and one loaf a week. She owned a cottage, and had two sons who lived with her rent free. They were both well-to-do, and had but one child between them. They allowed their mother thus to be a pauper, and the Guardians encouraged them by continuing the relief, and not requiring them to do anything or even pay for their lodging.

As bad a case of this description of error in administering the Poor Law as ever came before me was the following : A man presented himself at a Board of which I was a member and asked for relief. He was a widower with six children, and he said he could do nothing for his own support, owing to his suffering from asthma, though he walked about freely and did not strike one as being very ill, nor had he any medical attendant. Several of the children were doing something; and one daughter, who was quite young, was a remarkable singer. She had shown such talent that a subscription had some time before been made in order to train her, and she now earned on his own showing £3. 3s. a week. From inquiries it appeared that probably this was very much below the truth; she was single, and all she allowed her father was 8s. a week, though several Guardians remarked how very well the daughter had behaved in thus helping her father. The Board continued to allow a trifle of relief, though it was obvious that out of such large earnings, the girl (who appeared to have everything supplied her, besides her wages) could have easily maintained her father and assisted putting out her brothers and sisters who were growing up. Why should she do more, however, and save the rates, when the Parish was willing to give relief?

Very often it happens that persons apply for relief in the hope that the Guardians will take upon themselves the trouble of summoning the children, in order to make them refund to the Union part at least of the cost of their support. When this is done the House is usually given, and out-door relief should almost invariably be refused. The following is a case in point. A woman who had several sons, all of whom declined to keep her, applied to the Board for relief, hoping that it would take steps to compel the sons to aid her. She said she worked for four hours a week at cutting up rags, and that her earnings were but three shillings and sixpence a week for this. The Work-house was offered her, and the Board said it should take what steps it thought fit about taking proceedings against her sons. This seemed to suit her, or she made as if it did, though of course she had applied for and hoped to get out-door relief.

When cases of this sort come before the magistrates the action of the Bench is not always satisfactory, nor do they invariably support the Guardians even when they should. No doubt it is unpleasant for a magistrate to tell a man earning small wages, and with children, that he should do something for his aged parents, but it is essential that everything should be done to promote the habit of children assisting their parents, and not saddling them on the community. If anything indeed the law does not allow a wide enough circle of relations to be responsible for their worn-out connections, and I cannot but think that married daughters, grandchildren, and even nephews and nieces, should, if they are in good circumstances and their own natural feelings do not prompt them to do what is right, be compelled by law to help to support their own flesh and blood.

The action of the Guardian in all these cases is simple. First indeed, as in every transaction, must come the rigid investigation, and if then it is found that the children are able to support the parent wholly or in part, out-door relief should be refused, and in-door relief given, and steps taken against the children to make them refund the cost of maintenance. It may be said why not give out-door relief and take proceedings against the children, and so not punish the old parent for the fault of the child ? This would be a mistake. First because a great many cases would disappear by simply offering the House. Many children, though having no pride as to their parents receiving out-door money, nor seeming to care much for their privations, object to their going into the House, as they think that would be a reflection on themselves, and secondly because it very often happens that the parents and the children understand one another, and are conniving together in order to get as much as they can out of the Parish. The only way of breaking up this arrangement is firmly to offer the House and decline out-door relief.

PART III.

OUT AND IN-DOOR RELIEF IN ORDINARY
CASES.

N the judicious distinction in the administration of out-door and in-door relief depends almost the whole efficiency of the Poor Law as at present established by law. Nothing will strike a new Guardian of the Poor more than the slight circumstances which often decide Boards as to the form in which relief shall be given, without regard being had to any fundamental principle or systematic rule of action. Indeed his Union will be a favoured one if he does not soon detect anomalies and serious inconsistencies in the awards of his brother Guardians. He may even be disposed at times to fancy that the distinction which is made between granting out-door and in-door relief is often very slight and depends somewhat on the fancy of the Guardians at the particular moment at which the relief is made. Not unfrequently the considerations of the person's family, and the expense which he or she would put the Union to, if the House were really enforced has as much to do with the decision as anything else. The particular characteristics which should decide the question as to whether in or out-door relief should be granted, are however of the utmost consequence. The wishes of the individual applicant should not be considered, nor the immediate cost to the Union, but the abstract question as to whether, judging from the circumstances of the case, its previous history, and its present position, it will be the more likely to be permanently benefited by the one or the other form of relief. Nor is this all, for the consequences of the relief on others must be considered also, that is whether or no certain vices of which the natural effects are personified in the applicants are likely to be encouraged or discouraged by one form of relief or the other, both in the persons themselves and among the inhabitants of the Union generally. I propose, therefore, to take some of the common every-day cases which occur, and to consider the form of relief which it is desirable to grant to them.

CHAPTER VIII.

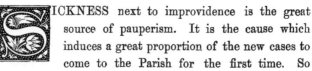ICKNESS next to improvidence is the great source of pauperism. It is the cause which induces a great proportion of the new cases to come to the Parish for the first time. So common indeed is it that persons hardly look upon medical relief as anything but a matter of course, and they rarely regard its receipt as really placing them on the list of paupers. The new Guardian will be surprised to hear how half or rather three-quarters of the cases are disposed of by the relieving officer simply saying " Illness of the man," " Illness of the woman," as the case may be, or perhaps only " Medical relief." After these magic words, the aid is granted without any discussion or further consideration.

The reason why this state of things has come about is from the idea being prevalent that sickness is one of those troubles to which mankind is heir, and which no amount of foresight can prevent, and no amount of care on the part of the sufferer can arrest. This is true to a certain extent, but from another point of view it is altogether a fallacy. The sickness itself cannot be provided against, or arrested in most instances by the individual, except of course in cases of reckless living and so forth, but the pecuniary privations and medical attendance required to alleviate the consequences are easily provided against. It should indeed be the business of the new Guardian to do his utmost to promote an extension of the thrifty habit by which all should provide when in health against the consequences of illness, come when it may. At the same time it is not surprising to find that so often no provision whatever is made for sickness by those who do not object to come to the Parish, when it is remembered that the Parish medical relief is so easily obtained. As this question is so important and involves such large consequences to the Parish and to the community, it will be as well if I draw attention first to the provision which even the poorest can make against illness and its consequences, and secondly to the proper action of the Guardian in granting out-door medical relief.

The only way in which sickness and its consequences can be guarded against is by a system of Insurance, that is, a setting apart by a large number of persons *while in health* of a small sum weekly or otherwise, so that out of the funds thus created the doctor's fees may be paid and an allowance granted to those who are so unfortunate as to be ill and to require it. This is the system adopted by all Clubs, Friendly Societies, Trade Societies, and so forth ; and, to their great credit, hundreds of thousands of our countrymen belong to these provident schemes.

Some may say that the very poor cannot afford to do

this, and possibly some cannot secure the allowances which most of the Clubs and Friendly Societies give their members. The number, however, who could not do so if they really tried, and if they cut off a part only of the amount now wasted in the public house, is but small. I am so bold, however, as to say there is not an able-bodied man, who, if he had a mind, could not provide at least for the medical relief. A sum of one farthing a week for himself and each of his family would do this. In a Union* where I once made careful inquiries, this farthing a week all round would have raised a fund more than three times as large as that paid to the doctors for the whole Union medical attendance. In a family of twelve this is only two pints of beer a week, not a very great tax. As long, however, as the parish medical relief is so easily obtained, it is not likely that even this slight tax will be willingly and voluntarily imposed.

The next point to consider is what the new Guardian shall do if he wishes to improve the existing state of things. In the first place it will be necessary as a preliminary step to promote the establishment of the means by which the poor may provide at least medical attendance for themselves in sickness. It would be cruel suddenly to abolish out-door medical relief and to leave the very poor themselves, after being so long accustomed to it, to find the substitute. The substitute must be provided in the shape of a Provident Medical Dispensary, and then the action of the Guardians may as an indirect compulsion oblige them to make use of this institution.

Here the co-operation with charity will be found of im-

* 'The Seven Ages of a Village Pauper.' Chapman and Hall.

mense advantage (chapter 29). The Charity Committee can
far better than any other body establish a system of Provident Dispensaries. It must be very simple. Many doctors,
particularly in suburbs and small towns, have already
Medical Clubs. These may be formed into branches if
wished, or left if preferred as they are. In each district
a room must be obtained for a certain time, each week
or each day, at which patients can come and see the doctor,
and where a certain number of drugs can be kept. One
member of the Charity Committee should attend some
evening, generally Saturday or Monday, to receive the
members' fees, which should be paid monthly in advance.
The doctors will then arrange the times of their visits at
each place, and this information will be printed on the card
of membership.* Cases of severe illness would of course
be visited by the doctors at the patients' own houses, but
others would come to the Dispensaries. The terms of
membership should be very low at first. I would strongly
urge a farthing a week per head as a commencement. It
is true that this sum will not be permanently enough, for
many can easily afford much more, but to make the movement popular it is essential to put no obstacle, such as a
high fee, in the way at starting. It is easy to raise the
amount afterwards when the Dispensary is at work. Besides this, it is obvious that to induce persons themselves
to pay something is the important consideration. It is not
so much the money obtained as the fact that a growing
habit of forethought and thrift is being thereby established.

* See 'Provident Knowledge Papers,' No 14. Parochial Dispensaries.
Chapman and Hall.

E

It is better indeed for the Parish at first, still to supplement the doctor's remuneration than to allow matters to continue as they are.

When this has been accomplished, and a fair machinery for enabling all to provide for sickness at this low rate has been established, the new Guardian should endeavour to induce the Board after a due notice, say six months or a year, either bravely to abolish out-door medical relief except to the aged, or to grant it only in very exceptional circumstances and then on loan only. To make this last arrangement (see chap. 30) the mode of payment to the doctor may be changed, and made into a fee per visit. Of course at first, if the new Guardian were so fortunate as to carry this reform, some care would have to be taken and considerable discretion exercised to prevent great complaints. If, however, the charity of the district were in harmony with the Board and with the movement, this would soon be overcome. It might be wise to give a person one or two warnings perhaps, or even at first to continue to grant the out-door Medical Relief on loan to a few undeserving cases, rather than to raise unnecessary opposition before the system had been at work long enough for all to see the advantages which it possessed. After a time all but the worthless would understand that the system was one of mutual benefit, the poor would be saved by thousands from ever coming on to the Parish, the pauper roll would be immensely reduced, the work of the Guardians would be lessened and at the same time the benefit to the community at large would be greater than could at first be possibly expected.

I would venture then to urge on all new Guardians that

they should aim at the abolition of out-door Medical Relief (except to the aged of the present generation), and promote to the utmost of their power the establishment in its place in every Union of a complete and self-supporting system of provident dispensaries.

CHAPTER IX.

PPLICATIONS of some sort or another from widows are almost sure to come before the new Guardian at the very first meeting which he attends. This difficult branch of relief cannot be shirked, it must be boldly faced, and the question what is the best means of treating pauper widows, and by what process can they be relieved, to secure the greatest advantage to the widows themselves and to the Union generally to which they belong ? practically answered.

In the first place it must be remembered that there are widows and widows. The simple fact of a woman having lost her husband, though it must be sad in the abstract, is not conclusive evidence that she is deserving of liberal or permanent out-door relief solely on that account. Widowhood must not be taken alone one way or another, but the circumstances must be investigated just in the same manner as if the husband were living.

To begin then with a respectable woman with a large family, hardworking and industrous, whose husband is suddenly cut off, and she left to do the best she can with her young children. Suppose investigation only shows her to be more and more an object of pity. She has never been on the Parish before; her husband belonged for years to a club, she has had the club money, but it will only just bury her husband, pay necessary expenses and keep her a week or so while she looks about. What is she to do? In years to come it may be hoped that by increased education such cases will be rarer from a habit of life-insurance extending to the artisan class. In the meantime, however, what is the Guardian to do with the case before him? The woman must be relieved and out-door relief must be given as liberally as possible. Then comes the further question is the out-door relief to be given in perpetuity? Is she to regard it as an annuity for the rest of her days or until she marries again? I fear that in most cases there is no help for it, but to regard such a widows' relief as permanent until all her children but one are able to earn something. The case should, however, be carefully watched, and as soon as each child is old enough to earn something, and certainly directly each child leaves school, the amount of relief granted to the mother must be reduced.

This is more important than may at first sight appear. I have come upon many cases (such for instance as at p. 23) where really the aid given to respectable widows has tended to prevent them urging on their children to do as much as they might to obtain some steady and regular employment. They know the relief will be reduced when the children are at regular work, and so they keep them hanging about doing nothing, or only odd jobs which are not likely to attract the attention of the relieving officer. This has a

twofold evil, firstly the children learn deceit, and secondly
they get into habits of indolence which are perhaps never
eradicated. A deduction should therefore be made in the
relief given to the mother, whether the child is at work or
not, when it is of an age to be employed. There can be
no difficulty in finding work for a child; and a parent
on the Parish should not be too particular so long as the
child can get a respectable occupation, however humble it
may be. As soon as all the children but one are off the
widow's hands, then, if she continue well and strong, the
Parish money may be and should be stopped, for an able-
bodied woman can and certainly should keep one child.

This action, as it seems to me, is the only practical action
which a Board of Guardians can take in such a case as
this, under existing circumstances of Society, and under
the present Law. True, if the charity of the district is
organized and in harmony with the Guardians (chapter 29),
the treatment may be very different. Such a case as I have
supposed, may be saved by such a system from ever coming
on to the Parish at all. In the first months of widowhood
some occupation may be found, which may render the
woman independent. A loan to purchase a mangle, or
to start in some business, may, if the woman has qualities for business, put her once more in a position above
requiring aid. Some special occupation which the Charity
Organisation may know of in the neighbourhood, may be
just the thing for her, or by the machinery of the organisation work may be known of in some distant part, and a
small loan may transplant her and her family to the spot,
to work and live on in independence and respectability.
All these assistances which are far better than any amount

of relief or alms may be given by charity, and especially by organised charity, but cannot at present be attempted by Guardians in their official capacity.

Let me consider now a more common sort of widow, one whose husband has done nothing to provide for the future, who has been making good wages, but who has been on the Parish whenever out of work or whenever he has been ill. What is to be done with such a case when the father is cut off? As a rule at the present time such an applicant obtains relief just as readily, nay, even more so than the first case. She is known to the Guardians and the relieving officer, and the password, " widowhood," is sufficient to secure her what she wants without any further inquiry. Looking, however, deeply and disregarding the individual, I doubt much if such action is the way to reduce these sad cases to a minimum. I cannot help thinking that it promotes improvidence and a reliance on the Parish among many men well able themselves to provide for their families in case of their death. Further, that the children of such widows are most likely in their turn to follow in their parents' steps, and, like them, to provide nothing for themselves, but to rely on the Parish on every emergency.

One mode of dealing with such widows is that of taking charge of one or more of their children, and leaving the mother with only one or two, or such a number as she is able to bring up without any aid from the Parish. Such a course is objected to by many persons as being unnatural and inhuman, but if the Workhouse has an efficient school where the children will be properly brought up, I believe that such a plan is by far the best. It prevents the mother becoming a pauper, induces her to earn her living and secures that some of the children at any rate, are properly trained. On the other hand, I am bound to say that if the children are placed in such a Workhouse school as many I have seen, where they are simply trained as permanent paupers, I could not recommend such a mode of dealing with any case however bad.

If, then, this plan cannot be adopted either on account of the inefficiency of the schools or the disinclination of the Guardians, I fear that nothing remains but to grant the minimum of out-door relief possible for the family. The refusal of out-door relief altogether to such a case as we are considering, which would in theory be the right step and perhaps the kindest, looking into the future and upon the system of relief as a great whole, would I fear in the present state of public opinion not always be approved. The Organisation of Charity would, however, come in here as in the former case, but in a very different manner. Such widows as these, even though they might be allowed out-door relief, are certainly not worthy of alms. At present, however, they are the very people who as a rule absorb so much from the alms of the benevolent of all denominations, for they know full well how to use their widowhood as an excuse for a perpetual dependence on doles. This should be stopped. The organised charity in the district, working with the Guardians, and in fact investigating these cases and recommending that the minimum out-door relief alone should be granted, would be quite sure to debar them from obtaining alms, as well as Parish money. By this means many would gradually be taught thrift, and to understand that reckless conduct during the years of comparative prosperity, would debar them from enjoying the same comforts in distress as the careful and the prudent.

There is a third class of widows, however, which is unfortunately not at all an uncommon one. These are utterly reckless, drunken and almost hopeless creatures, whose homes have for years been the abodes of misery, and whose whole example to their children has been such as to render their permanent failures, both socially and morally, almost certain. Not a few of these get out-door relief when they become widows, but such a policy is a wholly mistaken one. If a widow, with children, has been living in such a state, it is the greatest cruelty to the children to allow her out-door relief, and thus to encourage her in her mode of living, and in continuing as an evil example to the children. Even drinking to excess should be enough to cut off the out-door relief from any one, but especially from a widow with children. So far from trying to prevent her coming into the Workhouse, in spite of the cost every effort should be made to compel her to come in, in order that her children —for she herself is of little importance compared with their future—may have some chance of being rescued by proper teaching.

The new Guardian will, I hope, see that in the treatment of widows more has to be considered than their widowhood. All turns on the thorough investigation of their antecedents and present mode of life, and he who will wisely administer his Union, must carefully remember this. Perhaps the injudicious relief of few groups of cases, does more permanent mischief than that so often given as a matter of course to widows.

CHAPTER X.

DESERTED WIVES AND THEIR TREATMENT.

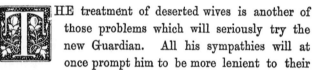HE treatment of deserted wives is another of those problems which will seriously try the new Guardian. All his sympathies will at once prompt him to be more lenient to their applications for relief, and even in those cases where faults may evidently have been on both sides, he will see that the woman is usually left with all the burden of the family, while the man takes himself off to enjoy alone his comparatively large earnings. In truth, at first a new Guardian may be led to treat a deserted wife almost as tenderly as if she were a widow, and not to be too particular as respects investigation into the circumstances of the case.

Without wishing to be too severe, applications from deserted wives require to be looked into, and their treatment usually demands a much firmer hand than at first one's sympathy might suggest. As a rule, the cases divide themselves into three classes; first, those who are really pitiable creatures, and where the husband has deserted

from his own wickedness ; secondly, those whose desertion
has been caused by continual quarrelling, at the root of
which is almost invariably drink on both sides ; and thirdly,
those who are in collusion with their husbands, and who
are really only trying to impose on the Union by making
desertion a plausible excuse for obtaining out-door relief.

The treatment of each of these three cases will of course
be very different. The first no one will say should not
receive consideration. They will be found, however, to be
scarce. No deserted wife must be placed in this category
as a matter of course. The strictest investigation must be
made, and nothing taken for granted. Not only so, but if
out-door relief be granted for a time the relieving officer
must continue to watch the case carefully. If finally it
proves to be really an instance of the first class, the woman
should then, and not till this has been fully established, be
treated as if she were a widow, as in truth she virtually
is.

The second and third classes will require altogether
another treatment. I must say from my experience I
think it will be found that the second class of deserted
wives is by far the largest of the three. Not that this
consideration excuses the man from his unnatural conduct,
but from the Parish point of view it makes all the difference
in the way they should be relieved. Domestic quarrelling
caused by drink on both sides, although pitiable, indeed
forms no claim for special consideration or relief, for if it
did it would be a practical encouragement of it. Whenever it is found that a deserted wife is known to drink, or
that the domestic circle before desertion was one of
perpetual strife, out-door relief should not be given, but

the Workhouse alone offered. If it be accepted, no pains or cost should then be spared in trying to find the husband and bringing him to justice. A large sum thus spent is well spent, for one example of a successful discovery of a deserting husband and his severe punishment will do immense good throughout the Union.

The same system, but with even greater rigidness, will, of course, be pursued towards the third category, namely, those who make-believe to be deserted, but where there is collusion between the man and the woman. These cases are by no means uncommon, but they are often difficult to detect, particularly where the relieving officers are few, and each has a large area or a very dense population to look after. When discovered, however, a note should be carefully made against such specimens, (chapter 28, d.) and no out-door relief of any sort should from that time forward, under any circumstances, be allowed to either man or wife.

If the above considerations are kept in mind and acted on, and above all if a rigid investigation be made of each case of a deserted wife before out-door relief is granted, Guardians will soon find that applications from this class will not be very numerous. The treatment also of those who come before the Board, which is at times now found to be so difficult and so hard to reconcile to one's feelings, will be simple and just, and in the long-run by far the most merciful.

CHAPTER XI.

DRUNKENNESS AND ITS TREATMENT.

HE granting of out-door relief to persons known to have been drunkards and who have become paupers in consequence of drink is quite unjustifiable. Where, however, persons are still addicted to intemperate habits the continuance of out-door relief is absolutely wicked, and the least evil is that the grant is nothing more than a subsidy out of the rates to the publican. In spite of this, cases frequently occur, and, strange as it may seem, many Guardians do not appear to regard this habit as an absolute bar to out-door relief. On one occasion, "She does not drink so much as she did," I heard remarked by a relieving officer as a sort of reason for being lenient with a woman, and out-door allowance was continued, though, of course, it should never have been granted. The same action I also saw pursued to an old man of seventy-seven, who was known to be a regular drunkard, his failings were proverbial, and he was taxed with being *almost habitually* as "tight as a drum." Again, I may mention an old woman of seventy-three, and her husband about the same age, who applied for a continuation of out-door relief. It appeared that they both drank very freely, and were rarely sober whenever they received money. I proposed the House, as it was evident that the relief merely went into the publican's till. My motion was seconded, but no one supported it. The out-door relief was continued out of consideration for their age !

Scarcely a meeting of most Boards of Guardians passes without such cases as these coming up, and this most serious encouragement being given to drunkenness. Instances might, in fact, be given without number. I feel convinced that this action is usually adopted in consequence of insufficient consideration, for the absolute duty of stopping out-door relief in all cases of drunkenness must be but too obvious to any one who thinks of the subject carefully for a moment.

Every Guardian who wishes to do something to reduce the misery of poverty and drunkenness should watch carefully these instances, and in every case decline all out-door relief, without considering the number of the family who will come into the House and the financial consequences to the Union, whenever the poverty can be thus clearly shown to be allied with and a consequence of drink. A consideration I have more than once brought forward applies here very forcibly, and that is the future of the children. Even if a large family be brought to the Workhouse, it isf ar better and far cheaper in the long-run to put the parish to their cost, than to allow them by a trifle of out-door relief to grow up with the wretched example of drink before them.

CHAPTER XII.

 POINT which will strike a new Guardian will be the extravagance of many who appear as applicants for the parish dole. Widows are especially noticeable in this respect. I may mention one whose husband had died by an accident on the Great Western Railway three weeks before she applied for relief. She had received £12 from a club and had spent £8 of it in taking the body a considerable way into the country to bury it. Nearly all the £12 was already spent, so 3s. and 4 loaves a week were given her. In the second instance the applicant was also a widow, said to be completely destitute, with a baby eight weeks old and five other children. The baby's clothes were embroidered and quite expensively got up, and the general attire of the family was superior to many a well-to-do person. 4s. 6d. and seven loaves a week were here granted.

The ease with which relief is obtained, and the uniform rule of granting widows the Parish money with but few questions and less investigation, has no doubt not a little to

do with this. Alms, however, may also promote it, for not
a few persons are very injudicious in the way they make
gifts to the poor, and promote habits which cannot tend to
the permanent comfort or happiness of the recipients.
Widows, however, are by no means the only offenders as
regards this extravagance. Well-dressed applicants of all
classes appear not unfrequently before the Board and ask
for relief. The new Guardian will be struck with the kid-
gloves and fashionable bonnets of persons who assert that
their only means of living is a day's charing a week at 1s.
6d. and food. It may seem hard, but such cases should for
their own good, to say nothing of the unfairness to the
hard-working ratepayers, be refused out-door relief.

CHAPTER XIII.

IMPOSTURE IN ILLNESS AND ITS TREATMENT.

 COMMON peculiarity of the applicants for out-door relief, which very few who enter newly on the duties of a Guardian will not fail to be struck with, is that sick paupers rarely "get better." If a case comes up, and the wife or relation appears for the sick person, that person is usually "worse this morning, please sir." No doubt it often is so, but the universal condition of getting worse is remarkable. The relieving officer may have seen the invalid the evening before sitting up, but to a moral certainty will it be found that now he must keep to his bed, he is so much worse. To an unsuspicious nature this is strange, but to a suspicious nature it is very suggestive. Suggestive of what? Is it not of the premium we set upon an exaggerated statement? Does it not show the knowledge that exists throughout the country, that probably we shall be too indolent further to look into the matter, and that we shall most likely grant help all the more readily and perhaps the more freely from this statement without taking the trouble to find out and to punish an imposture even though we may suspect it.

I was much amused on one occasion with a woman who, on being taxed with looking well, replied in great dudgeon, " I may look 'arty, sir. I'm not so 'arty as I look." On another occasion I remember a relieving officer stated that a woman's husband was somewhat better last week, on which the woman who was applying for relief replied sharply, " He's very bad. He's dangerously ill, sir."

Whenever this phase appears in a case, I will not say that out-door relief should be refused simply on this account, but it should be granted for at most one week, and during that time the Parish doctor should be required in all cases to visit the invalid, and to make a special written report of his or her condition. If this is objected to, and it often will be by the invalid, then the out-door relief should be absolutely put an end to.

CHAPTER XIV.

THE SPREAD OF CONTAGIOUS DISEASE AND ITS TREATMENT.

HE granting of out-door relief to cases of extreme poverty when afflicted with some contagious illness, is a matter of very serious moment to the community at large, and one which every Guardian, and especially a new one, would do well to consider. Sometimes indeed the applicants are so ill that it is impossible to move them, but often this is not the case when they first apply, and a trifle of out-door money is given them simply because the Workhouse has no separate building fit to be used as a contagious ward.

The first point then is the absolute importance of erecting some such building for a contagious ward—every Union should have one. It should be altogether away from the Workhouse, and it should never be used for any ordinary case, so that it may be ready on any emergency and at a moment's notice. Very often when a ward is nominally set apart for contagious illness, it is filled whenever the House is a little crowded, and consequently it is never available when wanted.

Whenever there is extreme poverty and such a building exists, out-door relief should be refused, if it is possible to move the patient. This should be done, firstly, because the chances of recovery are immensely more in the patient's favour when thus properly attended to ; and, secondly because of the safety of the whole district. No class of patient is so apt to spread an epidemic as a very poor one. He cannot be isolated, the clothes and furniture cannot be properly disinfected or destroyed, and the chances are they continue to be used and to infect others in all directions. Every Union should also have a proper conveyance for such cases. The expense may appear alarming at first, but it is not only in the interest of the poor but of every ratepayer as well, that precaution against the spreading of such disorders should be taken.

The following typical case came before my own observation. A woman who was laid up with scarlet fever applied for relief through the relieving officer. It appeared that she had one child some ten years of age, who acted as her nurse, assisted at times by the people in the house where she lodged. The officer also stated that almost everything, except a sort of bed on which she lay, had been pawned. Two shillings and two loaves a week were granted to her! and, strange to say, the woman recovered, though what her sufferings had been and to how many others she spread the contagion it is impossible to say.

CHAPTER XV.

 CUSTOM exists in most Unions which will puzzle a new Guardian not a little, and that is, the giving relief to non-residents. It has some connection, indeed, with the law of settlement, for non-residents are persons who do not live in the Union to which they belong, but receive relief through the agency of some other Union in which they have taken up their abode. As stated in another chapter (chap. 38), a person does not become legally a part of a Union until he or she has lived in one of its parishes for at least a year without ever coming on its rates for relief. Paupers, however, like others, are fond of change, and sometimes prefer to live away from their own district (and from their own relieving officer), particularly if it makes no difference in the relief. The law gives Guardians discretionary powers to allow relief to non-residents if they think proper to do so.

There are two classes of these non-resident paupers which will come before the Guardian. Firstly, those belonging to his Union and who live out of it; secondly, those not belonging to his Union who live within its boundaries. The relief is usually given in both cases by the relieving officer in the Union where the pauper lives, but the outlay is refunded quarterly or half-yearly by the Union to which the pauper is chargeable.

The usual effect of this arrangement is as follows :—The Union paying the relief cannot look after the cases, for it is impossible to send the relieving officers perhaps half across the country to visit them ; and even if the pauper lives near enough for the officer to go by a local train or omnibus, the Auditor disallows the expenses of his travelling. The Guardians and relieving officers where the pauper does live do not visit or look after the case, for they have little or no interest in troubling themselves about paupers whose cost does not come out of their own pockets. I have often heard the remark, " Well, we don't pay it," which certainly is somewhat suggestive of the way these cases are looked after. Literally, indeed, as may be supposed, they fall between the two stools as regards investigation and supervision.

The conclusion to which I have come as regards non-resident relief is, that it should be altogether refused. It is one of the worst forms of out-door relief, and is open to great abuse from the very imperfect way in which it is looked after. If a person wishes for relief, it does not seem unreasonable that he should live within the Union thus maintaining him ; and as long as the law of settlement remains, I would urge all Guardians to refuse relief except to those living within their own area, and who can be looked after in the usual way. If this rule is adopted it will be found that almost every non-resident case will disappear, for as a rule they are living with well-to-do relations, or are otherwise in comfortable positions. This is, in fact, almost invariably why they go away, so that they really are in no need of help at all.

CHAPTER XVI.

CASUALS AND THEIR TREATMENT.

ONE great difficulty which the new Guardian will have to face is the treatment of the casuals. This is one of the most unsatisfactory branches of his many unsatisfactory duties: according to the district in which his Union is situated, so will his experience vary. If he lives in a large town, he will find the House most beset with casuals in the winter. If he belongs to a suburban district, he will find the number increase in the spring when the winter-night refuges are shut, and when the tramps flock out of town, and trudge from one Workhouse to another, living as best they may by begging or stealing, but with as little work as possible.

The new Guardian should take an early opportunity of visiting the Workhouse in the evening, seeing the casuals received, and picking up what information he can from them. A few visits will well repay the trouble, and being a Guardian, he will of course have the right of seeing all that is going on. The scene which he will witness has often been sensationally described. I will not attempt to repeat

such an account of it, but will just state the usual procedure. The nightly ceremony commences with the iron gates
of the Workhouse being closed and locked, and around
them on the outside will stand the wretched objects who
crave a lodging. Some will have been hanging about near
the entrance for an hour or more, smoking their short
pipes, and talking of what it might puzzle the shrewdest to
guess. I have often thought as I looked at the groups, of
the words which should form the motto on every Workhouse,
" Let all who enter here leave hope behind." At the right
moment the head casual superintendent of the Workhouse
walks demurely to the gate, followed by the porter and
several pauper helps—

" When were you here last ? " he says, addressing a heap
of rags through the iron bars.

" Never been here before, sir."

" What's your name ? "

" John Nash."

" Don't think you have—stand on one side ; you there,"
he continues, addressing another man, " I know your face
well, you were here the other day, what do you mean by
coming again ? "

" It's six weeks ago, sir," replies the object, who of course
interprets the rule of not being allowed to come oftener
than once a month into a permission to come once every
four weeks at least.

" Don't believe it. I must look it up in the book.
Stand back."

So the officer goes on all round, separating not exactly the
sheep from the goats, for they all look too wretched even to
be the goats, but those whom he will pass from those whom he

intends to worry. Those whom he does not remember to
have seen before he makes stand on one side, and also those
he remembers by sight, if he thinks it is twenty-eight days
since they honoured him with a visit. The others he de-
tains, and if by any means he convinces himself that they
have applied within the previous month, they are refused
admission, and only let in after considerable discussion and
trouble, for it is doubtful whether he can absolutely shut the
gate on them for the night, whoever and whatever they
may be.

One of the paupers then unlocks the gate, and those fortunate ones who have been approved are allowed to pass in
and are sent two and two to the receiving ward. Here a
further investigation takes place. Their names are written
down and the places whence they come. They are made
to give up all matches, tobacco, knives, and such like
articles. They are asked if they have any money ; need it
be said that they never have ? Many of them really have
some money, but they bury it before coming in, or leave it
with a mate who stays outside. On one occasion, however,
the porter of my own Union found two half sovereigns
about one of the casuals. The man begged the porter to
be careful of his bad leg; this made the experienced
searcher suspicious, and he probed to the very bottom of the
pocket on the bad leg side, and lo and behold ! two bright
half sovereigns came to light. The man was ejected and
told to go and find a night's lodging at his own cost. The
valuables which are turned out on these occasions are
peculiar. They are supposed to be the entire possessions
of the owners, and as such perhaps are valued : combs, pieces
of string, tools, letters, tobacco, pouches of all sorts, rolls

of tobacco, knives, etc. On one occasion I even saw a piece of soap, and I could not help thinking something might have been made of the owner. After being thus searched, and leaving all their goods in the receiving ward, the casuals are marched across the yard to the baths superintended by the pauper helps. The clothes are taken by the pauper help and strung altogether with a long string through the button holes, and the men, on their coming out of the bath, are presented with a large stuff night shirt, and their own clothes are generally disinfected during the night. The water has been clean whenever I have seen the casuals bathe, and I cannot help thinking that the hardship of the dirty bath has been somewhat exaggerated. Be that as it may, the water has had good effect, for the Guardian will not fail to be struck with the cleanliness of most of the men; they are usually wonderfully more respectable-looking creatures with their clothes off than with them on. After the bath they are given their four ounces of bread, and locked up in the casual ward for the night. This apartment contains usually a long row of beds, or rather one long bed right down the room, with a number of dividing boards about three feet apart.

The classes of cases which the new Guardian will come upon by personal observation are numerous. I will briefly state some of my own experiences of different types of individuals which I have come across at the casual ward itself. One, I remember, was the type of a regular tramp, his very look was sufficient. I should say he had been a good deal in the religious line, for he had a sanctimonious way of looking at you, and moralised on what was said.

When another casual standing by bitterly remarked to me he would rather be transported than be a casual much longer, the first man replied with somewhat uplifted eyes, "That would be even worse."

Another class of casual one cannot help pitying and longing to look up their history with a view of doing something for them. I remember one in particular, he may have been an impostor, and very likely was, but I could not but think that there was something in him nevertheless. He said he had been a soldier, an artilleryman, that he had served in India,—he mentioned the places,—that he had been invalided after volunteering for Abyssinia, and that he had received a pension of eightpence a day for two years, that he had earned a living at his trade, boot-closing, since, but his health had been bad for some time, and he could not do very much, so that few masters would employ him. He went on to say that until a month ago he had worked at Woolwich for a man who was engaged by some regiment, but that the regiment and his friend had gone to Sheffield, and he had not the money to follow them. If he could but get there after them, he made out that his work would be continued. A tool he had with him somewhat substantiated his statement.

Another case I may give of a similar description. This man was a very well-spoken fellow ; he, likewise, may have been an impostor. He said he had been a waiter at the Queen's Hotel, Leeds, that he had had a row with his employer and had been dismissed. He assured me that the quarrel was in no way to do with money, but simply a disagreement. In consequence of loss of character he had been unable to get another place ; he had been obliged gradually to dispose of his clothes, and so in a few months he had come to be a casual. His manner was that of a waiter, and backed up his statement.

Some casuals take altogether another line, and are most amusing in their dignity. Not a few have an intimate acquaintance with the law, and a high notion of their rights. One strong hearty young casual who had been admitted to the Workhouse where I was, one summer's evening, on receiving his dry bread for supper brought it to the master and demanded that it should be weighed as he considered it short of the four ounces. He asserted that he had as much right to it and his lodging as any of the Workhouse officials had to their salaries. He knew the law, he was entitled to a quarter of a pound by Act of Parliament, they had not given it to him, and to prove it he insisted on its being weighed. The master accordingly got out the scales, and the crust was put into them; it just turned the quarter pound, whereupon the man took it back, saying that they treated him worse there than at the House of Correction.

A similar story may be told of another casual in a different part of the country. The bath in which it was usual to require the casuals to wash before retiring to rest was out of order. This was one of the large baths with hot and cold water laid on, and which are not surpassed by many in ordinary houses; it could not be used on this occasion however, so a stable bucket and towel was given to the man with instructions that he should wash.

"Do ye think I'm going to use that —— thing," replied the man. "The Hact o' Parliament says I'm to 'ave a bath with 'ot and cold water." No amount of persuasion would induce the injured dignity to degrade himself with the tub.

What to do with casuals is the point which the new Guardian will have to puzzle over. From my experience I would divide casuals into three classes.

1st. Cases of misfortune which should be relieved.

2nd. Cases of respectable but very poor men or families migrating for work.

3rd. Tramps and vagabonds in the present ordinary acceptation of the term.

As regards the first class I believe much might be done by a systematic organisation of charity working with the Poor Law (chapter 29). Take, for instance, the cases I referred to above. They occur daily, and if only a small percentage are telling the truth, much might be done to put them on their feet again. If they were willing to remain while investigations were made, and the truth of their stories was substantiated, that alone would be hopeful. If their story was correct, a few shillings on loan, or as a gift, the loan of clothes, or some other means might permanently rescue not a few from a life of degradation. In the two instances, out of many, I give above this would have been the case if they were really deserving, but no machinery existed to find out about them, and no one seemed to care to take the trouble to do so. If their story was untrue they might be treated as tramps and vagabonds, or even, one might suppose, be brought before a magistrate for trying to obtain alms under false pretences.

As regards the second class, namely, those who are migrating in search of work. This is a class which must be treated, if *bonâ fide*, with consideration ; one regrets that such persons when migrating permanently should be obliged to go to the Casual Ward, and were charity organised properly in all districts such things would not happen. Charity funds would be forthcoming for this, not as gifts, except perhaps in some cases, but as the recipients would prefer, in loans to be repaid gradually when circumstances were favourable. Indeed, many employers would be glad to advance, and in some cases do offer to advance money for the journey of extra hands when an organisation is to be found in the locality able and willing to see to the sending of the workpeople.

Besides those who thus permanently migrate a large number rest at the casual wards when migrating periodically for haymaking, hopping, harvesting, and so forth. These should not, strictly speaking, come to the casual wards, the extra wages they earn should enable them to pay their way to and from their place of work. Until, however, a higher social standard has been developed among the agricultural classes, higher remuneration obtained, a greater spirit of thrift instilled, and the present pauperising influence of out-door relief among so many far better off than themselves stopped, it is expecting perhaps too much from them to hope that they will absent themselves from the casual wards and provide their own board and lodging on the way. The Guardian may regret to see these, but anyhow for the present he may be content not to be too severe upon them.

We then come to the third class of casual, the tramps and vagabonds in the present meaning of these words. No organisation of charity can help them, and nothing but the strictest discipline is of any use. At many places I have seen these casuals employed indolently cutting wood, and the reason given is that it pays better than stone breaking. This I think a mistake. The young strong fellows should be required to break stones even if the stones don't bring in as much to the Union funds as the wood. The idea of stone-breaking will prevent many a rascal from coming in at all. To this class the present system is a great deal too lenient. They often do not mind the work given them, if they find it hard they refuse to do it, not actually defying the rule, but passively wasting their time till eleven o'clock, when they are free to go. They know very well that they will not be compelled to do their task. They understand that it is much easier for the Workhouse officers to get rid of them than to have them up before a magistrate because they won't work, and so consequently the work of the casual ward is a perfect farce as far as they are concerned.

The only means of dealing with these cases which I think will ever be of any avail is, as far as I can understand, not legal, except under the peculiar circumstances of a casual coming more than twice to the same casual ward within a month. There seems to be no reason, however, why it should not be made legal. From watching them a good deal I have remarked that the only moment when their faces display any life, and when they move with quickness, is that at which the word is given for them to leave at eleven o'clock. I infer from this that much as they like the night's shelter they are only too glad to go. I, therefore, strongly suspect that if in all these cases the Master of the Workhouse were empowered to keep them, say two or three days, or, better still, if he were allowed to give each man so much land to dig, or so much stone to break, a good two days' work say, and that all able-bodied casuals of this class would be detained until that was absolutely finished, and finished properly, it would not be long before this section of the casual visitors became much less numerous than it is.

In one respect the management of casuals differs from that of other paupers, and that is in the fact that permanently to reduce them depends not on any one Union, but on the efficiency of all the Unions over the whole country. At the same time these people know full well which places to avoid; tramps and vagabonds will keep clear of those Unions where hard work is enforced with the utmost rigour of the law.

The new Guardian should therefore bear in mind with reference to the Casual branch of his duties, that nothing will tend to reduce the deserving cases more than a systematic organisation of charity working with the Guardians, which may snatch not a few, as it were, from the verge of permanent pauperism and abject degradation. Nothing, on the other hand, will frighten away the indolent vagabonds so much as imposing on them hard work, and sparing no trouble or expense in making them do their utmost for the bread and shelter which they get within the Workhouse gates.

G

CHAPTER XVII.

ANOTHER difficult and at the same time most serious consideration is that concerning the management of the mothers of the illegitimate children born in the Workhouse. Some few married women come to the house to be confined, but they are the exception. As a rule when the mother's name only appears in the register it is pretty clear that the birth is illegitimate. When the father and mother's names are given thus, *John and Mary*, it may be presumed that the parents are married. The births in one Workhouse where I made inquiries were as follows :—

        1871, Illegitimate 22; Married 6.
        1872,   „   15;   „   4.
        1873,   „   22;   „   3.
        1874,   „   13;   „   4.
        1875,   „   20;   „   4.

The number in this Union, the population of which was 70,000, was not so great as at many others, but even taking only 20 per annum as an average out of every 70,000 inhabitants, it would make the annual number of illegitimate births in the Workhouses of England, not less than 7000.

These cases are among the most painful which come before a Board, and to a Guardian unaccustomed and not yet hardened to the sight, it is very sad to see women, many of them almost children, standing under such circumstances before a body of men. On one occasion a poor creature of but twenty summers was before us under these circumstances, but she already had a child three years of age. In another case at a distant Union at which I was present the unhappy mother was but fifteen.

When the mother and child are well, the usual routine follows of the mother applying to be discharged, when clothes for the child are supplied, and a shilling and a loaf is given. I have often seen two such cases at one meeting, and even three and more apply for admission or discharge. Some of the circumstances are most distressing. They generally say they have no friends and no home. One who applied to leave, told us she was going to take lodgings! What could that mean? What else could she do? A girl of seventeen, with a baby on her breast, with no home, no friends, one loaf in her hand and a shilling in her pocket!

The question then arises what is to be done with such cases? But this question is a good deal easier asked than answered. In the first place the Board should always, even at great trouble and considerable expense, take means if possible to affiliate the child. Of course if the mother absolutely refuses to state who the father is, it is almost impossible to do anything. When, however, she states who he is, and he can be found, and the fact can be proved, no means should be left untried to compel him to refund the cost and to take on himself at least the financial consequences of his conduct.

One of the great uses which would be found in having a systematic harmonious action between the Guardians and the organised charity of the district (chap. 29) would be to take steps to reclaim these wretched cases. True, much caution is required ; and no mistake can be greater than so to treat persons who have fallen as to make the very fact of their falling a help to worldly advancement. This is a direct encouragement to the very evil which we wish to reduce. At the same time it cannot be right for charity to turn her back on the unfortunate girl of sixteen or seventeen years who has gone astray or been deceived for the first time, and who we know full well on leaving the Workhouse with her burden of shame, can have no possible means of livelihood but by continuing her immoral life. The majority of these cases are penitent after the first fall, and would hail with delight any means by which they could regain the lost ground. Organised charity could do much here, not by pandering to them, not by treating them as if they were objects of exceptional commiseration and deserving of luxurious consideration, but with firmness, giving them opportunities for work, shielding them from the dangers and temptations which must first beset them when they are once more thrown on their own resources, weighted with the results of their first error. Giving them, in fact, an opportunity to redeem their position by their own efforts and by these alone, instead of allowing them as so many do now, to rush headlong down the abyss of wretchedness and crime, impelled by despair, and goaded on too often by the revilings of those who should be the last to throw a stone at them.

One very important and most essential mode by which charity can help these cases, and give them a chance, is by taking care of the infants during part of the day or during the time the mother is at work. It is obvious that the Workhouse cannot allow a woman to leave her infant and go out and seek work. She must either stop herself with it or take it with her whenever she passes through the gate. At the same time, a young woman often not yet over strong, cannot get work with a baby in her arms. Even if she can get something to do, the earnings will be very small, and no one will take charge of the infant for nothing, and no stranger will take an infant on any terms from a casual passer-by. Organised charity could, however, do much here. Work could not only be found for the mother on her first leaving the Workhouse, it might be unpleasant work, and it might not be the best paid sort of work, but it would be honest labour ; but an arrangement could be made by which the infant could be taken care of during working hours, and precautions could also be taken to prevent any attempt at desertion on the part of the mother, even if she had a mind to do so.

Another function which organised charity could often accomplish with great benefit is that of acting as a mediator between the fallen and their parents or family. Often these girls are afraid or ashamed to let their parents know anything about themselves. At other times parents refuse to see the children who have brought disgrace on their old age. This may be understood, though often such conduct hurries the wretched daughter with even greater rapidity down the fatal path. Charity could often gently and tenderly and gradually bridge over these chasms, and so reclaim many who now fall but to fall hopelessly again.

Sometimes cases occur in which a Board of Guardians does attempt in a somewhat rough fashion to promote morality by means of the Workhouse test. I have seen not a few instances of this description. On one occasion, I remember a widow of forty, having two big children, applied for out-door relief on the ground that she was about to be confined. The relieving officer strongly urged that it should be refused, and that the House only should be offered to her, as he was pretty sure that such a step would lead to the marriage being hastened between the parties concerned. The Board did as was suggested, and I believe in this instance the desired consequence followed.

The more the new Guardian becomes acquainted with these different cases, the more, I feel sure, will he become convinced that the only way of meeting them with any chance of success, that is, with any chance of reducing them to a minimum, is by the action of organised charity working with the Guardians. Working, too, not sentimentally but practically, with great kindness but with firmness and wisdom.

CHAPTER XVIII.

MISCELLANEOUS IN AND OUT-DOOR RELIEF EXPERIENCES.

THE new Guardian must be prepared for strange unexpected cases. He will often be called upon to decide questions of no small difficulty, to draw inferences from strangely conflicting statements, some of which will puzzle him as to whether in or out-door relief should be granted. He will, in fact, require at all times his best attention and no small amount of care and wisdom, if he hopes to do the best he can and to act consistently and justly.

One serious error let me warn him against, and that is one by no means uncommon, namely, the habit of reversing decisions previously arrived at as to the relief to be given to any applicant. Of course the importance of most careful investigation (chap. 28) cannot be too much dwelt on, but after a decision has once been come to, it should not be changed except under very special circumstances. Nothing is more pauperising than the fact being known that it is a habit of Guardians to change their minds if only the applicant be persistent enough. It induces

persons to come up over and over again until they get
what they want, if for no other reason, because of their
importunity. As one example out of many that have come
before me, let me mention that of a man of twenty-eight,
said to be weakly, but who was known to have hung about
the " Coach and Horses " for many years. He had repeatedly applied for relief and had been offered the House, but he
would not take it. He preferred his life at the " Coach and
Horses." At last after persisting in his application for some
years he was successful, and out-door relief was actually given
to him. On another occasion I remember exactly the same
thing was done, although the relieving officer stated that
the House had been repeatedly offered to the man, who
would not come in. Nothing can have a much worse
influence on a Union generally than such a mode of
administering relief. It must be obvious, that if the
circumstances of the case are not changed, one or other
of the decisions was incorrect. If the first was so, it
must have been arrived at without proper investigation ;
and if the second, then it announces to the whole Union
that a pauper has but to worry the Guardians enough in
order to get what he wants.

A strange phase which may strike not a few when first
attending the meetings of the Board, is the matter-of-course
way in which applicants seem to calculate on the relief
coming to them and the little trouble they consider
necessary in order to secure it. Sometimes so sure are
they of getting what they want, that they allow the least
possible excuse to save them the trouble of applying
personally, and are content to send, as it were, a message
through the relieving officer. On one occasion I saw a case

of a man of fifty-six, who sent word that he was prevented from coming because of the east wind. He was quite well, and the relieving officer reported that he was fully able to come, and that no doctor was attending him nor was it necessary that any should attend him. In spite of this he was given liberal out-door-relief ! It cannot be a matter of surprise that people rely on the Parish money so regularly when it is to be had so easily as this, and I would strongly urge that in all cases, unless a medical certificate be sent certifying that the parties are absolutely unable to come, no out-door relief be granted.

The expression of feeling on the part of the pauper, whether of approval or the reverse, which often follows the announcement of the nature of the relief to be granted, must not be taken as in any way indicating the real condition of the applicant, though a Guardian may at first be misled by it. Sometimes the gratitude of the applicant on being told the amount which he or she is to have, indicates that even more than was expected has been secured. I have heard them exclaim, " God bless you, gentlemen," though more often they look disgusted and grumble, and not unfrequently argue the matter and try to obtain a more liberal allowance than the Board is disposed to give. When the House is offered, an exhibition of temper is common and cases of great insolence are not unheard-of. Many, however, particularly the old hands, prefer the more dignified way of retiring with a toss of the head, saying but too plainly, " Thank you, sir, I'm above that." On one occasion a very disreputable widow with two children applied for out-door relief. She was told that nothing could be done for her but to give her an order for the House. " Then I must have it," she exclaimed, and walked out of the room.

Sometimes curious miscellaneous cases, showing strange phases of character, come before the Board. I remember a hale and hearty fellow who had no wife or children, and who could easily have maintained himself though he was sixty-seven years of age. He preferred however the dole of relief to which he had long been accustomed. He was well-known for having on one occasion remarked that he would always vote for the liberals *if they paid him for it.* Once he was refused out-door relief. He would not take the House, of course, but in a week or two he had got over the Guardians again, and was drawing his usual allowance.

The following is a peculiar case. A woman in regular employment, earning according to her own account 7*s.* a week, and lodging free, with a husband so feeble that for years he had been granted 2*s.* and a loaf a week from the Parish, applied for some one to be allowed by the Guardians to look after him and nurse him, as he was growing worse. The wife stated she could not perform the office herself unless she gave up the work and lost her 7*s.* a week. In this particular instance the Board decided that it would not do to give a nurse to a man whose wife was at work, but as a compromise the out-door relief was doubled. A new Guardian would certainly be puzzled with such a case, and undoubtedly the argument was illogical. If the man was entitled to relief at all, it is only right that he should have sufficient, and to suppose that it looks better to give extra relief instead of openly granting a nurse, is altogether weak and a low standard of morality. If the truth could have been got at, as it would have been by a rapid investigation, the chances are that the family could, with the charity and alms which no doubt they received in addition to the wife's earnings, have done without out-door relief altogether.

One thing the Guardian must always remember in dealing with pauper cases. He must never take anything for granted, or he may be sadly deluded. Here is a case. A man well-to-do deserted his wife, and after some trouble was traced, and a warrant issued against him. He, however, sent to say he would pay up everything if the warrant was withdrawn, and it was accordingly held in abeyance. Finding, however, that he was thus mercifully treated, he told his wife he would give her a shilling when he could, and nothing more. I need hardly say that the warrant was at once pressed, and his promises were not again trusted.

The Guardian of an ill-managed Union may at times be called upon to pay lodging bills, as happened in the following case. A man who was staying at an Inn was taken ill. He was soon out of money, and the relieving officer was directed to remove him to the Workhouse. The House was, however, too full, so that the landlord was requested to keep him, and the Parish accordingly had to pay the bill. The fault in this case was the insufficient Workhouse accommodation. This difficulty may of course occur at times in the depth of the winter, but it need hardly be said that under ordinary circumstances ample Workhouse accommodation, even though it be unused, as indeed it usually must be, is essential to an efficient working of the Poor Law by any Board of Guardians.

It may not be out of place to mention that the ages

of paupers as stated by themselves are not a little peculiar, and care must be taken in judging of them. On one occasion I heard a discussion arise as to the age of an applicant who came from the Green Island. The person would have it she was much older than she really was known to be, whereupon the relieving officer remarked, "Irish people never do know their ages." When people get on in life it is proverbial that they add at least two years every twelve months to their age. This is easily explained, for the relief is not only rather more liberal, but the older applicants grow the more likely they are to escape even the little inquiry which is at present made as to their history.

PART IV.

ANOMALIES AND PECULIARITIES OF POOR-LAW RELIEF.

CHAPTER XIX.

RICH PAUPERS.

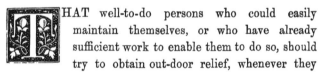

THAT well-to-do persons who could easily maintain themselves, or who have already sufficient work to enable them to do so, should try to obtain out-door relief, whenever they have a chance, is not very remarkable. It simply means their securing so much more a week for doing nothing; but that rich persons, so to speak, should willingly and from choice enter the Workhouse, and even die there, rather than spend their own money, is one of those mysteries which could never be believed, but from the fact that they have happened and constantly are to be met with still. The new Guardian will come upon such cases, and possibly even in his first year of office.

On one occasion, before I had been at a Board six

months, the master of the Workhouse reported that it had come to his knowledge that a woman had just died in the House, who was possessed of £30 in the Post-office Savings Bank. Steps were taken to secure this treasure to the Parish, as a return for the cost the woman had been during her stay. The poor creature, could she only have known, had had but the satisfaction of hoarding and denying herself during her old age in order that the Parish might spend her savings after she had gone. This cannot be called thrift, but approaches more the miser's characteristics.

I may mention perhaps the following instance, as it not only bears on this point, but it shows how little investigation is usually made into persons' histories, before they are given relief. One day a woman was brought before a Board where I was, by the master. Her face was bandaged up, and she had evident signs of having been recently in trouble. It appeared that she had been in the Workhouse for some years, and that a few days before she had obtained leave of absence to visit some friends, and had returned a couple of days after in the most deplorable condition. On further inquiries it transpired that she was in receipt of a pension of $2\frac{1}{2}d$. a day from the Patriotic Fund, and that this was the third time since her residence in the Workhouse that she had been to receive the annuity. No one however knew anything of this before. She had received on the day of leaving £1. 16s., which she said she had " lost in Hammersmith," but with part of which it was at any rate evident she had been drinking freely.

Several other cases have come before me in different

parts of the kingdom, but those I have given suffice to show that even within the walls of the Poorhouse unexpected treasure may be found. Of course nothing can be done when such cases come to light but to secure what is fair for the Parish as a return for the cost of the pauper. The moral, however, they tell, should be, that a more rigid and searching investigation of each case, an inquiry into the history and antecedents in a systematic manner of any person who applies for relief on which I venture so often to lay such stress (chapter 28), would render the existence of such melancholy specimens almost impossible.

CHAPTER XX.

AVING mentioned so much of the bad side of pauper life, it is but right that what can be said on the other side should be given as fully as possible. Cases of honest paupers do come before the Guardians, and the new member may at times be surprised at what he sees and hears in this respect. True when virtue is very much protruded we are apt to be shy of it, for everything that glitters is not gold. Cases, however, have come before me, showing pure and disinterested honesty even in the recipient of the Parish dole.

One of these exceptional instances was as follows:—A man with four children, who had been in the receipt of out-door relief for some time, informed the relieving officer that he was no longer in need of the money, and that it might be stopped. Stopped it was, and I never could discover any reason for the application, but one of real honesty and a desire for independence as soon as it could be obtained.

Another of a like nature, was that of an old woman, who stated that she did not now want so much relief as had been granted to her. She said that she still wanted some assistance, but could do with less from the Parish. Accordingly one of her loaves was taken off, and I scored the case down as one of sufficient note to be specially recorded.

Further examples might be given, but the above will suffice to show that there is a pleasant side even to out-door relief. Except to those who know the poor, and their mode of life, it is difficult quite to appreciate or to realise the amount of merit which is indicated in the cases I have given. The weekly income of both parties must have been indeed but trifling, and not too many even of the well-to-do class of life would voluntarily give up what they could continue to enjoy without let or hindrance. Such instances should make us charitable and raise our estimate of human nature.

CHAPTER XXI.

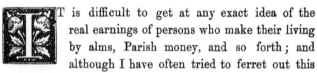T is difficult to get at any exact idea of the real earnings of persons who make their living by alms, Parish money, and so forth; and although I have often tried to ferret out this information in complete detail in individual cases, I have rarely been satisfied with my success. The recipients are close as indeed they need be, for they know that a continuance of their earnings may depend on their keeping their affairs to themselves. I heard of one case, however, and I noted it down at once, and it will be useful to give a new Guardian some idea of what is often encouraged by the present system of relief, etc. It is not a special case, but one in which the greater part at any rate if not the whole of the truth was got at.

The father made out that he was sickly, and either could not or would not do much. He had a wife and five children. One lady gave him half-a-crown a week; the clergyman gave him one and sixpence, and sevenpence for beer; the Parish money was three shillings and four shillings' worth of bread; the value of the extra Parish medical allowances was a shilling, and finally the Parish granted him one and twopence for beer, a luxury which in this case was considered necessary. The total 13*s*. 9*d*. was thus absolutely acknowleged, though probably several shillings more came in at times by accidental alms.

The wife stated that she earned six shillings a week. In addition to this, they had what the man could pick up by begging and such like, and some of the children earned something at crossing-sweeping, etc. Allowing therefore for all sources of supply, it is doubtful whether this family picked up in this indolent manner, less than 25*s*. to 30*s*. a week, or a larger sum than an industrious labourer would make at any honest work. To my great regret, out-door relief was continued. No one can doubt but that the children of this family will all be paupers, as their parents were before them.

If an organised system of charity worked in harmony with the Poor Law, as dwelt upon in another chapter, such cases would not be possible. As it is, they are common and should warn those who conclude that misery and a begging face is evidence of a deserving case for alms. It is not so, and a careful investigation is the only safe basis on which alms should ever be given.

The correct action for Guardians in these cases is simply to do all or nothing. If the previous history shows that the applicant has a fair claim for out-door relief, then the Parish money should be sufficiently liberal to prevent any alms being necessary. If, however, charity prefers to supply the needful, she should do it entirely and without Parish relief at all. For half-a-dozen

н 2

agencies to be relieving the same family is objectionable, even in a deserving case. Seeing, however, what it leads to with the artful, with imperfect investigation and with indiscriminate alms, it is obvious that a wise Guardian will, in the interests alike of the Parish and of the poor themselves, refuse out-door relief to those who are receiving regular relief from alms.

CHAPTER XXII.

PERIODICAL EXODUS FROM THE WORKHOUSE.

T certain periods of the year a sudden wish seems to seize a number of the old people to leave the Workhouse. When the weather is fine in the spring this is especially the fashion. Sometimes the most hopeless cases demand leave to go, and go they must, and do, though it is known perfectly well that they will be back in a few days. Others look so trim and brisk when they apply for their discharge that the wonder is why they ever came into the Workhouse at all. Healthy, strong, and intelligent-looking men often state on these occasions that they have been inmates for years, and only now apply to be discharged. The secret cause of most of these cases is, of course, that drink has brought them down, and, during their confinement, when sober habits have been forced upon them, they have recovered the manner and look which naturally was their own.

Old women are very much on the move at these times of the year. Many want to go weeding in the market-gardens, where they can pick up a few pence a day even when quite

infirm. Some expect, when they apply to leave the Workhouse, that they will get out-door relief to keep them,
and often they succeed. One old woman of 88 I particularly remember coming thus one day for her discharge. She
was determined to go, and strongly urged her claim for
out-door relief, which, however, was refused. She had been
in the House on and off for many years, and every now
and then insisted on leaving, only to be brought back in a
few hours in a most pitiable condition. Of course, however,
the Board had to let her go, for, very properly, no power
can detain any one in the Workhouse against his wishes.

These periodical applications are often encouraged by
the habit which many Boards adopt of giving a trifle to all
who leave the House. Of course, this rule is proper in
some cases, and the gift of a shilling or two and a loaf on
an inmate leaving, may not always be objectionable. It
sounds well thus to encourage people to go away, but it
is extremely foolish to make a rule of it, and to give
to cases who ought never to have come into the Workhouse at all, or who, it is evident, are only leaving to return
in a short time. With these last it really means a sort of
holiday fraudulently obtained at the Parish expense; and
not only this, but it often ends in serious bodily suffering and
misery to the poor creatures who, by long residence in the
Workhouse, are utterly unfit to look after themselves, and
who, probably, getting intoxicated with the money and with
what is stood them outside, often return in the most
woeful plight.

Another consideration which this subject brings up, and
for which the new Guardian should be prepared, is the way
the humanity of the Law is imposed upon when people

leave the Workhouse. It is impossible, of course, to send a man or woman away in a state of semi-nudity, even though they may come in in that condition. This is known, and, consequently, a plan, by no means uncommon, is for a Pauper to come into the House with barely a rag to cover him. He stays a short time and then asks to go out again, hoping to secure by this means some new clothes. It does not follow that these sharpers have no clothes when they come in, but they "plant" them, as the technical term is, among various friends who, of course, share somewhat in the plunder secured by the sale of the new garments. Most Unions are alive to this, though they cannot help sometimes being caught, and inexperienced Masters may easily be taken in. The plan usually adopted is to send such people away with a make-up from the worst deserted garments remaining in stock, those, in fact, which have covered some equally disreputable creature on his arrival. A stock of these elegant garments forms always part of the "properties" of every Workhouse.

CHAPTER XXIII.

INJUDICIOUS ADVICE.

FREQUENTLY the Guardian will find that injudicious advice has been the cause of persons coming on to the Parish. By this I do not mean the advice of paupers to paupers, but that of persons who should know better, such as clergymen, district visitors, and others. Some of these well-meaning persons seem to think that the Parish money should be obtained whenever it can be, and that a person not having it, even if he does not absolutely want it, is being treated in a sort of unfair manner, if he can make out a claim equally good with those who do enjoy the Parish dole. Two typical instances will be sufficient to show what I mean.

A woman of 62 who had kept herself hitherto, applied for relief. She was hale and strong. After some cross-questioning she let out that she had not thought of applying, but that one of the district visiting ladies had told her she should do so. The lady had stated that the rates were intended to keep old people, and that she could get

Parish money for the asking. The Board wisely offered the Workhouse, in this case, which I need hardly say was not accepted.

The other example is that of a woman having £15 a year of her own, with two sons earning 30s. a week each. She was ill and likely to remain so permanently. One of the sons presented himself to the Board, asking it to take his mother into the Workhouse. On careful inquiry from him it appeared according to the man's account that the doctor had advised the brothers to get their mother into the Workhouse, but that they would be willing to pay a trifle towards the cost of her keep out of the £15. It was indeed on the doctor's suggestion that the application had been made. The request was very properly refused.

All who have any influence over the poor should be careful in the advice they give them. The idea that the Parish money is their right, is one which should never be encouraged. True, it is the right of every miserable pauper to have enough to keep body and soul together, but the clergy and those who help them, should inculcate the spirit of independence and promote the idea that no one should go on to the Parish until every possible honourable means of independence is exhausted. As regards Guardians, they should at once discourage such cases and rigidly decline to give them out-door relief.

CHAPTER XXIV.

DOMESTIC PAUPER LIFE.

SOME of the experiences of a Guardian will be found to be sadly full of the worst phases of unhappy domestic life. One of the most painful cases of this description I ever heard was the following : A poor woman of 35 with six children applied for relief. The husband was a Scripture Reader and had left her, and had run away with some other woman. She seemed a respectable person, and as far as her history had been investigated she appeared a deserving object. Every now and then her wretched husband sent some money *for the children*, generally 5s. at a time, in stamps; but where he was she had not for years been able to discover ; 3s. and six loaves a week was given by the Parish ; and although it is possible that there may have been faults on both sides, one regrets that such men cannot be got hold of and severely punished.

Here is another scrap from domestic life. A wretched-looking woman wished the Guardians to give her relief, and take proceedings against her husband. She had been so often to the Court that the magistrates evidently did not know what to do with her. The Guardians urged her to go home, and try to live peaceably with her husband, when she exclaimed : " He's broke me five 'omes," implying that he had sold up everything on five occasions. From her look, however, she did not give one the idea of being a remarkably meek creature herself, or one who would patiently and passively allow her home to be sold up. She was then told that if she wanted him made to help to maintain her, she should apply to the magistrates. To this she answered with indignant scorn. " What's the good o' going to the magistrates, they are about as much good as nothink ? There's no justice done in this 'ere Board Room."

Sometimes the strangest possible domestic cases present themselves, as, for instance, the following which I shall not easily forget. An old woman of 64, somewhat demented, attired in the most original of costumes, with a little hat on the top of her head, came before the Guardians. She had been married but a few weeks to a young soldier. The said soldier had since gone to Ireland, and wrote telling her he was laid up in hospital, so that he was only allowed to draw a little money for tobacco. She said she had known him for four years, and that he was a steady man, so she had married him. The object of such a marriage is very difficult to detect. The woman besides being old was half silly, and it did [not appear that she had had any money, though possibly the man may when he married her have thought differently. She was given 2s. and a loaf, and has continued ever since on the Parish books, and will probably do so to the end of her life.

As regards the correct action in domestic cases, as little interference as possible should be exercised. The case of deserted wives I have considered elsewhere, but, generally speaking, when great family dissent and quarrelling is met with, the fault lies as much on one side as on the other, and it is a very safe rule to refuse out-door relief, and to take the whole family into the Workhouse. Out-door relief will only add to the cause for dissension. The man will want the Parish money, and the woman will not be satisfied with the bread; this will lead to endless disputes, and the children as they grow up, will get more and more accustomed to such sad scenes of domestic strife, and become more hardened in vice and misery. If on the other hand the House be given, and parents avail themselves of it, the children will for the time at any rate be removed from the evil atmosphere in which they have been living. Further than this, it is possible that the temporary judicial separation between the man and woman may have a beneficial effect, and rekindle domestic affections if the spark be not quite extinguished.

CHAPTER XXV.

S the establishment of crèches, where infants are taken in and nursed during the day while their mothers are at work, is a somewhat fashionable movement at the present time, it may be interesting to give an example or two of the way these things are managed by the poor themselves. In the charitable crèches it is usual to make some small charge, but this fee does not in any way cover the entire cost of the children, nor does it supply them with food, which is given away gratis, Alms have to supplement the parents' payments, and this is justified by the statement that the mothers cannot afford to pay more than the small fee asked.

With crèches kept for profit, of course this idea is not entertained, and the habit of mothers placing their babies with women to take care of them while they themselves are at work is common. Many of the poor, indeed, prefer to send their children to a neighbour in this way rather than to a charitable crèche. These nurses, if such they can be called, are frequently on the parish, though the sums they charge are very much higher than those which charitable ladies and clergymen are accustomed to ask. In the benevolent crèches, fourpence a day, to include attendance and food, is thought to be a high payment. I have seen many cases before the Guardians where this fee would include nothing in the shape of food. On one occasion a woman who did this work as a business, and kept a number of children, charged sixpence a day for merely taking care of each child, the food being supplied by the parent in addition. In this case, as in the others, out-door relief to the holder of the crèches had been granted, and was continued as a matter of course.

So attractive, indeed, is this business, and, strange to say, so readily do parents thus dispose of their children during the day that, on another occasion, I saw a woman who was an inmate of the Workhouse, apply to be discharged with the express idea of becoming a crèche-holder. She was of somewhat feeble intellect, but stated that she hoped to make a living, as she had done before, by a little needlework and taking in children to look after during the day while their parents were at work. She was accustomed to receive fourpence a day, she added, for these children, without giving them anything to eat. Milk or other food was supplied by the parents, in addition to the fourpenny fee. She was either not so fashionable a pauper as the rest, or possibly the condition of her intellect lowered her value in the market.

The conclusion which these and similar examples have produced in my mind is that it is evident that the poor (for it must be remembered that these women take charge

of the children of the very poorest) do not need to be still
further pauperised by the establishment of charitable
crèches. Possibly the attention which infants receive is
better in these institutions than with private persons. If,
however, this be the ground on which their establishment
is justified, and it certainly is a sounder idea than the
notion that the parents cannot pay, there would seem to
be no reason why crèches should not be established as a
business and made self-supporting, and not maintained by
alms. A ladies' visiting committee to see that the children
are properly looked after is really all that is required.

PART V.

PERMANENT REMEDIAL MEASURES.

CHAPTER XXVI.

THE WORKHOUSE SCHOOLS.

(a) *General Policy—-Separation from the Workhouse.*

NLESS the new Guardian belongs to a highly favoured district indeed, much of his best attention will be required by the Workhouse schools. The chances are he will find them contained in the Workhouse, forming part and parcel of that establishment, and combining all the evils which such an intercourse is certain to engender. He may see that they are almost hopelessly deficient, or at first sight he may think them fairly good, but in whatever state they are, the question as to whether they are being conducted properly and on the best system is one which the educated and intelligent Guardian should personally face. He should take nothing for granted, but look into every point himself. The efficient and judicious working of the schools is indeed of the most vital importance not only to the ratepayers of the particular Union, but to the community at large. However great a matter the proper treatment of *adult* paupers may be, it is trifling as compared with the training of the *young*, who, according to that training, are either destined to swell the ranks of useful and industrious citizens, or to add to the miserable roll of pauperism and misery which disgraces our country.

In.order to save the new Guardian some labour in hunting through the blue-books bearing on the subject of the proper treatment of pauper children, I will venture to give a short summary of the history of pauper education, and of the general principles which the highest authorities have laid down to secure efficient management.

Previous to 1834, children were herded together with adults, and received no training in the Workhouse except that of a vicious character from the older inmates with whom they were associated. Since that time this state of things has much improved, and the knotty point of deciding how much or how little these children should be educated has, ever since the introduction of the new Poor Law, been continually debated. While many feel that to give them a training better than that which an agricultural labourer can secure for his offspring is unfair to the ratepayer and a premium to pauperism, others look upon it as rather hard that children should suffer the consequence of a destitute condition which has not in any way arisen from their own fault. The wisest, the soundest, and, regarding it from the lowest point of view, the most economical

I

policy, is that which was adopted by the Poor Law Commissioners in 1836, who stated, "That the Workhouse children should be so taught as to give them the greatest attainable chance of earning an honest and independent maintenance for the remainder of their lives." This amounted tacitly to a recognition of the *policy* of employing every effort to depauperise the rising generation.

With this grand object in view all reformers have directed their efforts to a mitigation of the enormous evils arising from the association of children with the elder paupers in Workhouses. The 4th Report of the Poor Law Board for 1838 contains three long and most excellent reports by three of the Assistant Poor Law Commissioners, including Dr. Kay (now better known as Sir J. Kay Shuttleworth). All these reports urge the abolition of the schools in Workhouses, and the placing of the children in separate establishments formed by the association of the children of several Unions. Mr. Chadwick, another well-known Assistant Poor Law Commissioner, whose name is associated with all the improvements of the New Law, has urged the same thing very forcibly. At a speech he made on one occasion, when I recently read a paper on Pauper Education, he urged the importance of separate schools as the only means of improving efficiently and economically the condition of pauper children.

Mr. Tufnell, who for forty years has been engaged on this great question, and who has done so much for it, is of opinion, as he states strongly in his last report, that no other educational machinery has yet been invented at all equal to the large district school. In his report for 1871 (page 215, 1st Local Government Report), he lays down certain principles acknowledged by all authorities as essential for the proper training of pauper children, and deduces therefrom the following conclusions :—

1st. That the children ought never to be reared with adult paupers.

2nd. That they should always be brought up industrially.

3rd. That they should be instructed by efficient teachers.

4th. That the classification, and therefore the instruction, is more effectually carried out in large than in small schools.

5th. That it is proportionately cheaper to feed and superintend large than small numbers.

6th. That no school can be maintained in a state of efficiency in which the teachers are continually changing.

7th. That the chances of a pauper child earning an independent livelihood are proportional to the distance of its removal, when launched into the world, from its own low relations and haunts of vice among which it has probably passed several years of its life.

He then goes on to say that, " A very little consideration will show that every one of the above conditions is answered by the district school system far more completely than by the Workhouse."

In corroboration of this, Mr. Tufnell, in the same Report (page 221), gives the experience of the chaplain of the Brighton Union. This gentleman had held his office for twenty years, during which the children were kept in the Workhouse, and then he had six years' experience of the effects of placing the children in a separate establishment conducted on the district plan. Comparing the two systems, he says, "The character and history of the Brighton Workhouse children for many years is frightful to think of. I can remember as many as forty-four persons, inmates at the same time of the able-bodied ward, male and female, all brought up in the Workhouse schools, most of them thieves and prostitutes. Thank God, there is an end of this, or anything approaching to it. Of fifty girls sent out from our present schools, I only know one fallen; of about the same number of boys, the great majority are justifying the hopes of their teachers and the expectation of the promoters of this important charity. In Brighton, at least, society has shaken off a great scandal, and the ratepayers of the parish a heavy burden. Here, for the future, Pauper Schools will no longer be the nursery of pauperism."

Mr. Woodhouse, one of Her Majesty's Inspectors of Schools, states in his report to the Local Government Board in 1870 (22nd Report, page 135), "The reasons for which I myself advocate the erection of separate schools in all the larger towns, and the formation of school districts in less populous places are, first, that it is desirable to remove children from Workhouses in which the mere presence of adult inmates, apart from the question of contamination, familiarises their minds with the idea of a place to which they can return in after life whenever they find a difficulty in getting their own living, and thus renders it more difficult than it would otherwise be to implant in them habits of industry and self-reliance; secondly, because a far more thorough industrial training can be imparted to them in separate and district schools, and one more calculated to enable them to get their living in after life, either in farm service, in the army, navy, or mercantile marine, or in various kinds of handicraft ; and, thirdly, because this system would afford, at a comparatively small expense, a thoroughly good education to the children of the smaller Workhouses when the scanty numbers in attendance render it impossible to secure the services of competent teachers, and when the education which is given is at once costly and inefficient."

I may further remark that one of the objects for which the Metropolitan Poor Act of 1867 was passed was to secure the entire removal of the children from the Workhouses of the metropolis to district or separate schools (page 27, 23rd Annual Report, Poor Law Board, 1870).

Turning from the evidence of the Poor Law authorities themselves, let me refer to the Report of the Duke of Newcastle's Commission of 1861, than which no abler nor more impartial investigation of the subject of education has ever been made in this country. It devotes considerable attention to pauper education, and page after page condemns the system which we continue to cherish in so many, or rather in almost all our Unions, namely, that of keeping the children in the Workhouse. The Report dilates on the bad moral influences of Workhouses on children brought up in them ; it states that the schools destroy all spirit of independence, that the tendency of Workhouse training is to produce helplessness of character, and a loss of all desire for independence. The Commissioners endorse, in fact, in every way the opinion of the Poor Law Inquiry Commissioners, who state that, "The children who enter a Workhouse quit it, if they ever quit it, corrupted where they were well-disposed, and hardened where they were vicious."

Another point which the Duke of Newcastle's Commission goes into is the difficulty of getting good teachers in Workhouses. The teachers must be under the Master of the Workhouse, and this is a position which few good men will accept.

I might continue to multiply authorities, for, as the Report of the Duke of Newcastle's Commission states, evidence bearing on this view of the subject would be easy to increase to almost any extent. What I have quoted will be sufficient, I hope, to satisfy the new Guardian, as it did that Commission, that "Children cannot be educated in Workhouses in a satisfactory manner." If this be so, he will make it one of his main efforts to get the children out of the Workhouse, and to remove them entirely from the influence of the association of the place and of the adult paupers.

(b) *The Pauper Infants.*

Very few Workhouses have Infant Schools, and yet there are many thousands of infants at this moment in the Workhouses of the country. Most new Guardians will find a field for energy in this quarter. As regards the importance of Infant Schools little need be said, for it must be obvious to all that the tender years of infancy require careful treatment, and that those little ones who have, by cruel circumstances, been deprived of all the blessings of home need more than usual care and training to overcome the drawbacks with which they must enter upon life.

The infants in every Workhouse should, without doubt,

be formed into an Infant School, even including those of only two years of age, and this Infant School should be conducted in such a way as to combine physical with mental training. The difficulty, of course, would be to establish such a school with the comparatively small number of infants which are to be met with in many of the Workhouses, but this, so far from being an argument against infant pauper training, is another convincing proof of the importance, urged in the previous remarks, of combining different Unions, and of removing all children from Workhouses and placing them in organised schools.

The teacher of the infants should never be a pauper. This assertion may almost sound like a truism, and yet in very few Workhouses is any one but a pauper put in charge of the infants. It is usually some old woman who has behaved tolerably well in the House, and who has been there some time, assisted possibly by the last convalescent from the lying-in ward. The old woman very likely does not even know her letters, and her assistant, even if she be better educated, is not likely, particularly with her own child to look after, to trouble herself unsolicited much about the teaching of her other charges. Here, then, is a work obvious and simple for every new member of a Board of Guardians. He can go and see the children, he can, without much special training, detect whether the infants are being brought up properly, and he can, if he finds they are not, urge on his colleagues an amendment of the system.

In order to give some reality to these remarks I will recount as shortly as I can my own experiences in connection with the pauper infants of my Union. We had no

Infant School of any sort, though usually our children under seven years of age mustered about 20. On the first Wednesday of each month, that is, on a regular stated day, a Committee of the Guardians visited them. We found the little creatures generally arranged on the floor round the room, and on our entering, a cry of hurrah! was heard at a given signal. On these occasions, by the kindness of one of the Guardians, some sweets were distributed, so that a knowledge of what was coming possibly assisted the energy of this mild attempt at enthusiastic mirth. These children were looked after entirely by two paupers, one an old woman, aged 79, called 'Granny,' and the other a young woman of one or two and twenty. Granny informed me that she taught the children their letters; but I doubted if she were competent to do so, for she owned to only just knowing the *big* letters which were hung on cards around the room. On one day going into the adjoining room which was the sleeping apartment of all the children, I saw a baby of about six or eight weeks old, lying on the bed. The young woman took it up and said in the most natural and matter-of-course way, "This is my baby, gentlemen." I glanced to see if she had on a wedding ring, but of course there was none. On leaving the ward I asked the Master of the Workhouse if she were a married woman. "Oh! no, sir; that's her second child, the other one is in the House as well."

Finding this to be the state of our infants, I brought the subject, together with the general question of improving the school (p. 133), before the Board, but they refused to do anything, and not a single member would second my proposal for reform. I was not disposed, however, to take this as final ; and I would urge on all new Guardians never to take no for an answer, or to allow opposition, or, what is worse, apathy, to stop them in any reform which they may have convinced themselves is right and just in itself.

I should have stated that the quarters occupied by our 17 infants and two women consisted of two attics, the day room being 18 ft. by 15, and the night room 22 by 18, with a most offensive closet at one end. Both apartments had a sloping roof, making the height of the premises to range from 8 to 10 feet. Seeing the staff by which these children were managed, it struck me that to get them out into the fresh air must be a work of great labour to the young woman, for most of them would require to be carried down two long flights of stairs, and Granny could do little to help. I accordingly inquired into the subject, and to my amazement I found, on the 29th of July, that they had never been outside the Workhouse walls for nine months. The Master of the Workhouse owned to this, and indeed the date when they had been out last was a matter almost lost in the mist of ages.

It is to be hoped that the Union to which I belonged was an exceptional one, and that not many infants are in the state in which these children were. My action on this discovery was a strong one ; but considering that every proposition for reform in these very schools, and for these very infants, had been rejected by the Guardians, I knew that if I was to do anything for these pitiable children I must take decided steps. I accordingly wrote a letter to the 'Times,' recording the facts. If any new Guardian should venture to follow my example, I may warn him that this will bring a hornets' nest about his

ears, as it did round mine. The Board never forgave me,
but within fourteen months they passed an almost unanimous resolution to send the children to a District School,
a reform which the Poor Law Board and the Local
Government Board had been urging on them in vain for
fourteen years.

Few will, I hope, have to deal with such difficulties as
these. Few Guardians will absolutely support such abuses
when pointed out to them, but the danger is that men
who have been many years on a Board may resent almost
every proposal by a comparatively new member, and may
be as deaf and blind to obvious evils as the man who will
not hear or see. When this is the case the new Guardian
without regarding himself or what is thought of him at
the Board, must at any cost have the infants properly
and efficiently brought up.

There are three ways in which infants may be treated :—

1st. An efficient infant teacher may be appointed to
train them in the Workhouse.

2nd. They may be sent to a District School.

3rd. A cottage with a garden may be provided at a
distance from the Workhouse where all the infants may
be sent under the charge of some competent woman.

The first plan is the worst, though it would be an
obvious improvement on many Workhouses, and no Board
of Guardians can excuse themselves for not doing at least
so much for the infants committed to their charge.

The second plan is far better, but it is not possible for
many Unions immediately to adopt it. Of course, it may
be done gradually by a combination among a number of
Unions, but except in the neighbourhood of London where

District Schools exist, years might elapse before a country Board of Guardians, with the best intentions, could succeed in establishing a District School.

The third plan, however, which is the best, may be carried out successfully in the remotest Village Unions as well as in the densest town. The cottage or cottages should be removed from the Workhouse at least some hundred yards, or, better still, a mile or more, and the matron should be responsible to the Board direct, and not in any way under the Master of the Workhouse. Many an educated, kind, and motherly person would be glad to accept the office without a large salary. The children could go to the Village Infant School, and be further trained in mind and body by the home influences of the matron. They would be in the open air as much as possible, and as each cottage would hold but about ten or twenty at most, they would be brought up with an idea of home, and with all the advantages of individual care. Where more than one cottage was necessary, the casual children might perhaps be separated from those orphans and deserted infants who were permanently on the Parish. The cost of such a system would be a little more than the present mode of bringing up, but the benefits to the children, and consequently to the community at large, would be immense, and repay the outlay a thousandfold.

I would suggest to all new Guardians a consideration of these plans, and urge on them to do their best to induce the establishment of this last system, as an experiment at least, during their term of office.

(c) *The Workhouse Schools.*

The next point to consider is the School, that is, the Educational Establishment for the Workhouse children over seven years of age, where they have to remain until they obtain employment. Pauper Schools for elder children have received more attention, generally speaking, than the Infant Schools. For many years efforts have been made to improve the former. The fundamental fault, however, of the schools remaining in the Workhouse still exists in most places, in spite of its having been so often pointed out by the Poor Law Board itself, and consequently in but too many cases comparatively poor results have been obtained. Some 40,000 children are still being taught in the Workhouses of the country, and every new Guardian should make it his utmost endeavour to reduce this number.

In the first place let the Guardian examine into the teaching staff of the schools. This, as compared with that of thirty years back, is much improved. Still it is far from being what it should. But few good teachers will submit to act under the Master of a Workhouse, as they are obliged to do when the schools are part and parcel of that building. My own Union was a fair specimen of the results of this arrangement. From 1851 to 1874, that is, in 23 years, we had had 16 masters. Each had stayed on an average one year, five months, and one week. The salary we gave was not much, it is true, £30 a year and rations ; but this could not have been the only reason for their frequent leaving. How can a school be efficient with these constant changes ?

Again, as regards the strength of the teaching staff. In schools of a hundred or even more, usually but one teacher is to be found, in addition to the pauper helps. Proper progress cannot be made in this way. The consequence is that the elder children, themselves often very backward, are made to teach the younger ones. As an example of this, on one occasion in the corner of the room, where the elder girls were employed, either in knitting socks or in some other kind of needlework under the mistress, I found about ten younger children presided over by a big girl. She had a large sheet of little words with which she was supposed to be teaching her class their letters. I went up to them and asked the first to spell me a word, pointing to one on the sheet. The monitress put her finger to the first letter of it, but the child did not know what it was. I called the next child up, she knew one letter only. I examined several of them, and not one knew her letters. All this time the monitress kept her finger in a most remarkable way on this one word and under this one letter. I remarked that they did not seem to know their letters, and the schoolmistress then came up. Being perhaps somewhat suspicious, I spoke to the girl who had been acting as monitress, and said to her,

" I suppose you can read well ? "

" No, sir, I can't."

" How long have you been in the school ? " I inquired.

" About a year, sir."

" Do you know your letters then ? "

" Not all of them, sir," the girl meekly answered.

" And yet she is put to teach these children," I remarked to the mistress. " Surely this cannot be right."

" Well, sir, she is not the regular girl who teaches them," the mistress replied with some confusion. " Sally Jones does so generally, but she happens to be away to-day. The truth is, sir, this girl is a little gone in the head, and I thought she would keep the little ones quiet."

Even for pauper children the teaching staff must be efficient unless the school is altogether a sham.

Next, let the arrangements of the school and their connection with the portions of the Workhouse occupied by the adult paupers be considered. Probably, as in my Union, the Guardian will find that the children's quarters are not only close to the adults, but that they form even a passage through which the old paupers are continually passing; that the children dine with the old paupers, and what is even worse, that a number of the old paupers, both men and women, assist in the management of the children especially out of school hours. Nay, as has been already referred to, they even help in the teaching them if so it can be called. Let the Guardian carefully consider these things, and ascertain whether in his opinion such a training is likely to depauperise the children.

A third matter for the new Guardian carefully to investigate is the building in which the school is conducted. Air, light, and space are as important in the education of children as books and teachers, even more so, for without health the finest training is thrown away. Not only should the room be lofty and light, but the playgrounds should be such that the children can run about them. A small confined brick yard engenders marbles and such games instead of cricket, rounders, and other fine healthy and manly sports. In many Workhouses the schools have got wedged in somehow as if they occupied space which was begrudged them. The Guardian should indeed see to this. My own Union was exceptionally bad. The school premises had been condemned times out of number. The Local Government Board and the Poor Law Board Inspectors year after year for more than fourteen years had drawn attention to them, but the Guardians had insisted on retaining them and doing nothing to improve the children's condition. The Inspector in one letter from the Local Government Board even stated that " the defects in the school cannot be remedied by any improvement in the present buildings, and that nothing short of a radical change can be effective."

I give this to show what some Guardians may expect to find, although I hope that few districts will be found to be as unsatisfactory as the one to which I have just referred.

Another habit which a new Guardian may remark is that of employing the elder children to copy out the lists of applications for relief for the weekly meetings of the Guardians. Many of them do this well, and it may be said that it is good practice in writing for them ; the eldest boys also not unfrequently stand at the Board-room door, and usher in and out the broken-down creatures who apply for the Parish money. In themselves these duties are no doubt harmless, but they all help to stereotype the children as paupers, to make their one being and experience little else, to associate all their ideas with relief, and to familiarise them with the circumstances of pauperism, which it is most desirable should be kept as much away from them as possible. A new Guardian would do well to urge the abolition of these practices if he finds them existing, and to employ the elder paupers for these duties.

The practice of sending the children constantly on

errands during school hours should also be noticed. I
rarely indeed have entered the schools of my own Union
without finding some of the children away from this cause.
They act as errand children for the whole establishment;
and though no doubt in proper hours this is a very good thing,
yet constantly to take them from school for this purpose is
far from right. It is unfair to the teacher and most unjust
to the children themselves.

The next point is the absolute working of the schools
from an educational point of view. Here a new Guardian
may find much scope for his investigations. The ordinary
bookwork routine questions may be fairly answered, for it
must be remembered that the schools are inspected
annually by outside and highly efficient men. One of the
weak points, however, in bringing up children in Workhouses, particularly those who are orphans and who
remain there all their early days with no holidays or
friends or home to visit, where their minds may be expanded
by outside objects and thoughts, is that they never learn
the common every-day matters which children who run
about in freedom, however poor, are sure to pick up. Too
commonly also they fail to learn to apply what is taught
them, even in the simplest matters. They naturally
estimate everything by their own narrow experience, they
literally vegetate, and their minds remain about as ex-
pansive as the walls within which they live.

Take, for instance, the following examples from my own
experience. On one occasion I asked some Workhouse
girls about fourteen in number, whose ages varied from
eleven to fifteen, what bread was made of? About half of
them replied, "flour." But when I followed up the one

question by another, "and what is flour?" only one in the whole class could answer me, and then with great timidity and doubt.

"What is a spade?" I asked a class of boys from eleven to thirteen years of age. The answers varied; some did not know; about a quarter gave a fair answer; one said, "what they dig up 'taters' with;" another doubtful one, emboldened by this answer, ventured to say, "what they dig up cabbages with." On further inquiry this boy was sure that if it was used for 'taters' it would not be a spade. In the dictation they were doing, the word *metal* chanced to come with an explanation as to what metals were generally used for. In spite of this, not one child could tell me what they understood by metal; some said "gold and silver," not a few "money," and one thought "coin." They were unanimous in their opinion that an iron grating in the floor was not metal. I also asked them about the manufacture of bricks, as the district where the Workhouse was situated happened to be a brick country. Not one could give an intelligent explanation of the manufacture. One said bricks were "clay and straw," another "mortar and hay," a third "earth," and so forth. They knew bricks were "made to build houses of," but one lad of about eleven gave it as his opinion that houses were "built of putty." One of the elder girls once told me that the meat we get from a sheep is pork. This may seem strange, but it is not surprising when we consider that the child had probably been brought up all her life in the Workhouse and that a butcher's shop was a very exceptional sight to her.

On one occasion I asked the younger children, whose ages varied from seven to ten or eleven, several questions.

K

I found they could with but few exceptions count up to twenty, and that the elder ones knew the alphabet. As regards the number of their toes, however, they were not so certain, several had twelve and stuck to it—the number of fingers was an easier matter, as they could set to work to count them, which they did when asked.

The teaching of arithmetic is often sadly deficient. I once asked the eldest class of boys who were using the sign of plus + in compound multiplication what it was. They said "plus." On being asked to explain what they understood by this word they replied correctly, " a sign of addition." The explanation of the meaning of this expression only one boy was able to venture on, and his idea was that one plus two meant " one and carry two ! " I need hardly say that the whole point of the exercise they were doing was lost, and they could only have been working by a routine rule which they did not understand. Another day for the same class of boys I wrote a string of figures on the blackboard, and as a divisor put 10000 thus:

$$10000 \,)\, 66349456214 \,($$

one of the children did it correctly, working it through by *Long* Division. Not one had a notion of cutting off four figures, and several made the answer 0000. I then left the same string of figures and multiplied it by 22 in two lines, namely 2 and 11, and divided it by the same number 22, thus:

$$
\begin{array}{r}
66349456214 \\
2 \\
\hline
11 \\
\end{array}
$$
$$22)\overline{}$$

Two of them worked it out correctly, but not a single one saw that it was being multiplied and divided by the same thing. The teaching which this indicates is of course simply an attempt to make them work out a certain number of rules of thumb without in any way developing the intelligence. I may state that the class was composed as follows:—

2 boys of 10. One born in the Workhouse and one had been in four years.

4 boys of 11. One born in the House, one had been in 6 years, and two 3 years.

2 boys of 12. Both had been in about six years.

4 boys of 13. One had been in 4 years during the winter only, one 3 years, another 3 years during the winter only, and one 2 years.

Having now given some of the chief characteristic defects which are to be found in Workhouse schools, in addition to the all-important radical error of their existing in the Workhouse at all, the question will naturally arise what is the new Guardian to do after carefully investigating the condition of affairs at his own Workhouse? His first aim should be to get the children removed. This may be a great undertaking, but it will only require persistent effort. It may be done in several ways:

1st. By separate schools being built away altogether from the Workhouse.

2nd. By the children being sent to a District School, that is, to a school formed by several Unions.

3rd. By boarding out as many as possible in cottages at a distance.

4th. By sending as many boys as possible to some Training Ship.

There are advocates for each of these plans, and authorities differ as to which is the best. For my own part, I should like to see the fourth plan adopted in as many Unions as possible for a few boys, and also a very careful experiment of boarding out tried on a larger scale than has hitherto been attempted, though I cannot say that I am myself satisfied that this plan will ever answer as a general thing for all pauper orphans and deserted children. The bulk of the children, however, even if these two plans are experimentally tried, will remain to be dealt with. The best plan in my opinion is to build schools, to hold about one hundred children in each, *provided they are at some distance, a mile at least, from the Workhouse,* and altogether separate in management from it. The schools should be superintended by a teacher and a matron, an educated motherly woman even for boys' schools, and a staff of about one teacher to each 30 children. On the sub-committee of management formed by the Board of Guardians, there should always be a fair proportion of ladies, if this plan is adopted. But if the new schools are built close to the Workhouse, or, worse still, if they form a wing to it, however excellent the premises may be in themselves, they will be little better as regards their depauperising influences on the children than if they remained altogether in the Workhouse.

In places near London where large District Schools already exist, it may be preferred to send the children to one of these at a cost of about 1s. a day. This is a high charge certainly, but in the Workhouse itself if every item is included, it will be found that each child costs little if anything under 6s. a week.

If the new Guardian secures the removal of the children under any of these conditions from the Workhouse, he will have done great things, though he must not be disappointed at failure in the first or the second trial. The minor amendments of faulty arrangements, such as I have referred to in the Workhouse Schools, he may perhaps carry by degrees, while the greater reform is pending.

Without wishing to be egotistical, I will recount shortly my own experiences in this matter; which I give to show that if a new Guardian only exercises persistence even against serious and unusual difficulties he will, at last, accomplish satisfactory results.

Our schools were in every way objectionable, as I have stated. Every fault which could exist did exist, and in the administration of the schools, little could be pointed to as correct. The premises were small and low. The dormitories were over-filled and unhealthy, children slept two in a bed, ophthalmia and other such complaints were common, and for many years had been reported on by the Inspectors as being produced by the overcrowding and the other evils. The playground was a mere triangular passage, the old paupers looked after the children, and were mixed up with them in a way that was fatal to all hope of improvement. The drainage and water-supply was also bad and deficient, and the Government authorities had been year after year for fourteen years endeavouring to induce the Union to change the condition of the school, but to no purpose.

I was not long in finding out the state of affairs, and in bringing before the Guardians the arguments and facts in favour of a reform which I have ventured to lay before my readers. The result was a complete failure. They could not dispute the chief facts, but they cut the knot of difficulty by refusing to a man to second my motion for reform, and consequently stopped any discussion on the subject. I was not silenced by this, however. The circumstances I have related concerning the infants helped me, and the press took up the subject. The press is always ready to sift a matter to the bottom. 'The Times,' the 'Lancet,' and other influential journals investigated the circumstances and at last an official inquiry was held by two Inspectors. The main point considered was the creation of new schools or some better mode of disposing of the children. The chairman stated that the Inspector turned the Board-room into a "terrestrial purgatory," to which the Inspector replied, "The key of the new schools will unlock the gate of that unpleasant place." The other Inspector remarked that, "for four years longer than the siege of Troy, the Guardians had resisted successfully all changes in this (that is, the school) direction." The upshot of this inquiry was the formation of a committee to report on what should be done. This alone was a step.

Though I myself was carefully excluded from this committee, its being called into action was promising; but when the report was issued in a week or two afterwards, and stated in so many words that nothing should be done and that there was no need of present reform in the schools, the most sanguine might have almost despaired. In reality, however, it was the best thing for my cause. A slight improvement might have delayed reform for years, but a determined opposition to amendment after what had happened was certain to lead to a regular and sweeping change. For three months this report remained in a pigeon-hole at the Local Government Board, and in despair I was permitted by the courtesy of ' The Times ' once more to lay the facts before the public, and to urge on the Local Government Board to acknowledge either that their Inspectors had exaggerated the matter in every report or that the Board itself was powerless to do anything to stop the evils which had been pointed out to it.

On the very day on the morning of which my letter appeared, the Local Government Board replied to the report, whether this was an accident or whether it was cause and effect I leave my readers to decide. The letter among a number of points stated as follows : " As regards the children, the sleeping accommodation is for boys 52, girls 32, total 84, whereas according to the last return there are in the wards 119 children." The letter went on' " The Board proposes to issue an order forthwith fixing the number to be placed in each ward, according to the accompanying statement, and it will then be unlawful to retain in the wards a greater number. The Guardians must therefore at once consider what measures they will take to provide the additional accommodation which is so urgently required. With regard to the children's wards, although the Board will fix by their order the numbers to be placed in these wards, they are of opinion from the

Reports of their Inspectors that the wards are wholly
unfit for the reception of children, and unless the Guardians proceed to provide better accommodation for the
children, the Board will have no alternative but to issue
an order to close these wards. The Guardians in 1871
admitted the necessity of the Workhouse extension by the
purchase of land and by advertising for plans of schools
and other buildings. The removal of the children to
a separate building provided for them by the Guardians, or to
a District School, would allow of the wards now occupied by
them being appropriated to the adult paupers, and would
thus in some measure provide additional accommodation for
these classes. The Board request that the Guardians will
take the subject into their immediate consideration, and
that they will inform the Board what practical steps they
propose to take in consequence."

This thunderbolt, as may be imagined, caused not a little
excitement, and week after week it was considered until, on
the 3rd March, an order came from the Local Government
Board limiting the numbers to be put in each ward, and
declaring that after the 25th March it would be illegal
for us to house more than these numbers.

A second committee was accordingly appointed, and within
nine months of the day when no one would even second a
motion to consider the reform of the schools was the Board
discussing schemes and plans for the erection of large new
premises for the children, at a cost of many thousand
pounds. This scheme, however, was not adopted, but
within a year of the issue of the first report declaring that
nothing was required, the Board had almost unanimously determined to send, and a week or two after actually did send,

the children to a large District School a few miles from the Workhouse; the very place I had recommended in the first instance.

Few new Guardians can have much more discouragement than that I experienced in the above instance. I venture, however, to think that any new member finding his Workhouse schools in an unsatisfactory state, may, if he be but persistent enough, have them reformed, although I hope he will be able to succeed by more gentle means than I found necessary to employ. I have dwelt on the matter of schools at considerable length, from the conviction, as I have already stated, that their efficient management is the most important element in Poor Law Reform, and lies at the root of the permanent reduction of poverty and pauperism.

CHAPTER XXVII.

EDUCATION OF THE CHILDREN OF OUT-DOOR PAUPERS.

THE Education Act of 1873 provides completely for the education of the children of persons in the receipt of out-door relief. A compulsory law, in fact, has been passed on their behalf, and, as far as it goes, the provisions are most explicit, requiring every out-door pauper child to attend school. Unfortunately, Parliament, in 1874, thought fit to make the third standard of the Code the standard which should comply with the Act; and, after passing which, before the Inspector, pauper children need not be required to go to school any longer. This standard only includes the following amount of knowledge and the proficiency required to pass cannot be considered sufficient to overburden even a pauper child.

" Standard III.—Improved reading of plain narrative. The scholar to show comprehension of the meaning of the sentences read, and to point out the nouns, adjectives, and verbs.

(a) Five lines from the same book, dictated slowly by a few words at a time.

(*b*) Fair small-hand, with capital letters and figures, to
be shown in copy-books.

Notation and numeration up to 1,000,000. Four simple
rules. Money and time-tables."

The wording of the Act runs as follows :—

" Where relief out of the Workhouse is given by the
Guardians or their order, by way of weekly or other continuing allowance to the parent of any child between five
and thirteen years of age, or to any such child, it shall be
a condition for the continuance of such relief that elementary education in reading, writing, and arithmetic shall
[unless there is some reasonable excuse, etc.] be provided
for such child, and the Guardians shall give such further
relief (if any) as may be necessary for that purpose."

It may be supposed that this Statute is so simple that
the education of these children is an accomplished
fact, and that this chapter might be dispensed with.
Such a notion would be erroneous, however. Like every
other Act of Parliament it can be and is evaded. True, if
children do not go to school the Parish relief granted to
their parents is illegal, and should not be allowed by the
Auditor, and should be repaid to the Union funds by the
Guardians or relieving officers themselves. Even, however, if the Auditor does disallow sums thus wrongly ex-
pended, after a long correspondence they are generally
remitted by the Local Government Board. In the majority
of cases, however, the Auditor takes it for granted that the
children do go to school, and does not require proof one
way or the other on the subject, unless some troublesome
person persistently draws his attention to an irregularity.

In most Unions, no doubt, an effort is made to comply

with these regulations, but in very many the trial is not yet satisfactory, and it will need the new Guardian's careful attention to see that many of those very children who most require the provisions of the Act to give them some chance of getting out of their groove of poverty and ignorance, are not, from their very position, deprived of the advantages of education. To tell pauper parents to send their children to school is not enough. Even to threaten that if they do not do so the relief will be stopped is not sufficient, for if nothing more than this is done disregard of the law will be of every-day occurrence.

Let me give the following instances out of many which have come before me :—

A woman with four children applied for relief at the Board where I was sitting. The relieving officer reported that out of 100 days the children had been at school but 21 times. The mother said she told the children to go, and gave them the school pence. She certainly said she took no more trouble to see that they went, and it was evident, if her statement was correct, that the young truants spent the pennies and rarely entered the school. The Board continued the relief, however, and once more cautioned her; only, however, to be again deceived.

Another case was that of a widow who had an extra amount of relief given her in order to enable her to pay the school fees. In spite of this, none of the children had been near the school between May and August. Neglect on the part of the relieving officer is here evident, it is true, but still the fact remained, and the children were the sufferers.

Another case is worth mentioning as showing not only

what a dead letter the Act of Parliament may become which enforces school attendance on the children of those receiving out-door relief, but also how a loose way of administering it encourages deceit and falsehood, from the very earliest years. A woman who was deaf came before the Board and she brought one of her children, a little girl of about twelve with her as an interpreter. As we could get nothing out of the mother we spoke to the child.

" Have you been to school? "

" Yes, sir."

" Where? "

" At Hounslow," she replied with great hesitation.

" What school at Hounslow? "

" I don't know where, sir."

It further transpired that the child really never went to school at all, but had only just been inside once in order to be able to say she had been when asked by the Guardians.

The last case I shall mention shows, even more forcibly, how careful and persistent the new Guardian must be to prevent this law being evaded. A widow with two children was granted relief at an annual revision in May (page 174). An extra allowance was also made to her specially to pay the children's school pence. In the following August the relieving officer reported that, though the relief and the extra school relief had been paid regularly, the children had never been to school, and he stated further that there was no reason why they should not go. He was directed to bring the case before the Board again the next week. In the meantime the relief was continued. He did bring the case before the Board again, and it appeared the children still did not go to school; nevertheless, the relief and the extra school fee relief were continued. A third time the matter was brought up in September, and though the relieving officer repeated to the Board the statements he had previously made, and added that the circumstances of the case remained just as before, he was directed to bring the case up again the next week. In the meantime the relief was continued.

It will be said that here at least the Board was to blame. The difficulty, however, arose, firstly, from the absence of any proper machinery which would have rendered it impossible for this breach of the law to continue for more than a single week; and, secondly, from the unwillingness of the Guardians to take extreme measures, and to cut off the relief because the parent would not send the children to school.

In this case, indeed, the woman did not even urge extreme poverty or the necessity of retaining her children at home to aid her in getting a living. It was simply apathy and indifference, and the relief was continued from a mistaken wish not to be too hard on the woman.

Unless, then, some plan is adopted by which the attendance of the children will be secured as a systematic thing, it is obvious that the new Guardian will find that this wise act of the Legislature is in many cases a failure.

Two modes of accomplishing what is desired are sometimes suggested:

1st. The payment of the school fees of these out-door children by the Board of Guardians direct to the schools.

2nd. The granting of extra relief to the parent for the school fee, and the introduction of a card a copy of which is given to the parent for each child. This card shows the attendance of the child at school, and has to be initialled by the teacher each week. Unless it is produced duly filled up, the relieving officer does not give the relief to the parent, but requires the parent to appear at the Board of Guardians at their next meeting, and explain the reason of the child's absence from school. Exceptions are of course allowed in cases of illness, etc.

The objections to the first plan are obvious. One is that it in no way secures the attendance of the children at school, it merely secures the payment of the fees of those who are regular. There may, no doubt, be something to be said as to the advantages of this to the school, but it is evidently not sufficient of itself to satisfy the Act of Parliament, which states that the school attendance shall be the condition on which alone the out-door relief to the parents shall be continued.

Another objection is, that it takes away an important part of the parents' responsibility. It is highly desirable to maintain a spirit of independence and personal responsibility as far as can be, even among out-door paupers, and especially among widows who are largely interested in these arrangements. The giving of relief in any shape is more or less a species of demoralization, it is true, but to pay directly for the children's education, and to relieve the parent of the duty of looking after it, is a still more effective method of pauperising. Moreover, it is the establishing of another direct means of relief, which is highly objectionable, and likely to lead to complications. Suppose, for instance, a person's out-door relief were stopped, the question would arise, are the children's school fees to be discontinued? The person would say to a certainty that if they were, the children could not be kept at school. Hence the onus of stopping the fees and causing the withdrawal of the children from the school would fall upon the Board of Guardians, and gradually the only way to get over this would be to undertake the permanent payment of the larger number of the school fees in the Union.

Another point of no small importance as regards the welfare of the children themselves, is that the paupers would form a distinct class in the school. They would be different from their companions, and consequently a separate caste. This is undesirable, particuarly as they would be apt to be looked down upon by those who paid their own fees. Probably, however, this would die out, for their ranks, thin at first, would gradually and rapidly be swelled. Parents who temporarily went on the Parish would soon see the advantage of continuing to pay no school fees, and having this tax defrayed by the Union funds. In time, like Pharaoh's lean kine, they would as it were eat up the others, and those parents who never went near the Parish, would think it hard that they should have to pay for all their children, when their neighbours, because they were so improvident as every winter to require Parish relief, were allowed to send theirs without any cost to themselves.

The second plan, that of the card, and giving the pauper a slightly more liberal allowance, when necessary, obviates all these difficulties. It is a far simpler and better plan, and one adopted at the suggestion of the Local Government Board, as a means of securing the ends aimed at by the Act of Parliament. The card is very simple and may be printed as follows :—

———— UNION.

School Attendance Card.

Head of Family }
relieved.
         ———————————————————

Residence ————————————————————————

————————————————————————

NOTICE.

This Card must be kept clean and submitted to the School Master or Mistress, regularly every Monday Morning, for the insertion of the number of Attendances of your Child at School, and must be produced to the Relieving Officer when applying for your weekly relief.

Irregular attendance of the Child at School will result in your relief being discontinued.

Child's Name _____ *age* _____

Name of School _____

Date. Week ending	No. of Attendances at School during the Week according to School Register.	Initials of the School Master or Mistress.	REMARKS.
187			

Nothing can work more easily than this arrangement. The parent is told on the first application for relief, that all the children between five and thirteen years of age must be sent to school the following day, (unless of course they are ill.) A card is given for each child, and he or she is informed that this card must be brought the next week, when application is made for the relief, and that in the meantime it must have been filled up by the teacher, to show that the child's attendance at the school has been regular. The parent is warned that if this is not done the relief will be withdrawn, as the Guardians have no power to expend the rates unless this rule is complied with.

The only point to consider, is the trouble which this card involves on the teachers of the schools. This, though a small matter, should be mentioned. There are few teachers, however, who will not gladly perform this task, requiring as it will only a few moments' time each week to accomplish so important a result as the regular attendance at school of the out-door pauper children. It will also secure the regular payment of their fees, for if the Guardians give the proper amount of extra relief for the school pence, the parent can have no excuse for not paying them, and must be required to do so each week.

The new Guardian of a Union where this card system has not been adopted, and who suggests the introduction of this simple improvement, must not expect it to be taken to at once. Its establishment at my Board took almost as long as the reform of the schools. When first brought forward, every possible objection was raised to it. One member amidst the laughter of the meeting asserted that the first words on the card were enough to condemn it;

" It was to be kept clean. Could any child be expected to keep a card clean ? " Another was sure the children would play the truant, but it was difficult to understand how the cards could assist them in so doing.

Should the irregular attendance of the out-door pauper children at school continue in spite of his remonstrances, the new Guardian will have no other course than to lay the circumstances before the Local Government Board. To do this he should obtain the facts of one or two good cases. General statements are of no use. I was obliged to do this, and the Local Government Board eventually laid down the law very forcibly in reply to a letter from the Guardians which stated vaguely that the children " attended school where practicable." The Local Government Board stated " The Board (that is the Local Government " Board,) will only observe that the Guardians have no dis- " cretion in this matter. The child of every person in " receipt of out-door relief must receive elementary educa- " cation, unless the child can be brought within the " exceptions sanctioned by the statute, and it will be the " duty of the auditor to disallow the relief given to any " pauper where the rule of the statute is disregarded."

When this letter came another attempt was made to adopt the cards, but without success, and it was not till the auditor, in consequence of the correspondence with the Local Government Board, had disallowed some of the expenditure to parents whose children did not go to school that the card system was introduced.

The most difficult argument to meet in connection with the compulsory sending of these children to school, is the "starvation" one, which is often freely urged. The applicants themselves will say that if their children go to school they themselves cannot live. They not only cannot pay the fees, but they cannot spare the children, who help them to earn a living. Without them there is no one to look after the baby, to mind the home, to turn the mangle, and so forth. Many of these cases are merely specimens of the usual pauper grumbling; but no doubt there are families of the deserving and hard-working poor, on which it falls very hardly. These cases will be made the most of, to discredit the law and to stamp it as cruel. Nothing can be more unfair than this, however, for though the law is firm, and very properly so, for these are the very children whom it would be most unjust to deprive of a sound education—it provides that the Guardians may give extra allowances to make up for the losses thus incurred by the family.

The remedy then for hardness is entirely in the hands of the Guardians; but not a few who dilate on the harshness of the law shut their eyes to this provision, simply because they think it will increase the rates if carried out. The surest way of reducing the rates permanently is to educate the children, particularly of the hard-working poor, who, although circumstances have been sorely against them, and who have been compelled to seek the Parish dole, do their best to be independent and who thereby prove themselves to be made of the right stuff. Whenever this starvation argument is used let the new Guardian more carefully than ever investigate the case, and, if it be really a deserving one, urge a more liberal relief, rather than encourage the parent in depriving the child of the blessings of an early education.

Another warning I must give in connection with this

subject. It is not enough that the parent shall show that the child goes to school, but the character of the school must be considered. It must be an efficient school, and none but those under Government inspection should be recognised. The keeping of a school among the poorest class is often resorted to by unusually unfortunate persons who are absolutely incompetent, just as in the middle class the same occupation is taken up by decayed gentility, who are but too often equally unfit for the duty. At one meeting of a Board, I heard two out-door paupers, who, from their mode of talking, it was evident were quite ignorant, announce that they added to their Parish money by keeping a school of out-door pauper children. Such an arrangement is of course a farce and must not be allowed. The Guardian should make it his business to see that the present privation of the parents in sending their children to school is turned to the utmost advantage by their attending at institutions where their education will be efficiently conducted.

CHAPTER XXVIII.

THE RIGID INVESTIGATION OF EACH APPLICATION FOR RELIEF.

(a) *General.*

NE of the most fruitful causes of pauperism is the fact that in many instances out-door relief is granted without due investigation being made into the circumstances and previous history of each case. The chances are that the new Guardian will find, as I did, that his Union is no exception to this rule. If this be the case he cannot do better than agitate on the subject of the importance of a more complete and thorough investigation of each case, or urge too forcibly the necessity for a full written statement being given to the Board by the relieving officer, of the circumstances and previous history of each application which he presents for consideration, in addition to the special reasons on which the application itself is made.

The following may be the form of a resolution to lead to a discussion on this subject.

"That it is most important both in the interest of the poor as well as in that of the ratepayers, that relief, particularly out-door relief, should be given only after a most careful and searching investigation of the circumstances of each individual case of application.

That this investigation should not only be made by the relieving officer at the house of the applicant, but that a clear, short, and precise statement of the circumstances of each case should be made *in writing* by the relieving officer and presented with the application for relief.

That this statement should contain, in addition to the information now supplied as to the name and age of the applicant, whether married or single, and the number of his or her children, the following particulars :—

1.—Occupation.
2.—Wages when employed at ordinary occupation.
3.—Present earnings.
4.—Number of times the applicant has received relief, distinguishing out-door from in-door relief, and the half years in which he or she has received it.
5.—The amount of money thus received, and the number of days in the Workhouse.
6.—Whether the applicant belongs or has ever belonged to any Friendly Society. If so, its name, and when he or she belonged to it, and the reason for giving it up.
7.—Whether the applicant has ever taken advantage of the facilities afforded by the Post Office Savings' Bank or Penny Bank, or any other means of thrift.
8.—Whether the applicant has any relatives who are

legally bound to support him or her, and whether
such relatives are able to support him or her.

9.—Whether the applicant has ever been convicted of
any crime and if so the nature of that crime.

10.—Whether the children, if any, are legitimate.

11.—Any other information."

All these particulars are absolutely essential to enable
a Board of Guardians to form a just appreciation of the
merits of each case. Some of them it will be said are
indeed already supplied in the chairman's book, or can be
got at by asking the relieving officer for the information.

This is, however, a different thing from having a formal
written statement which can be referred to afterwards, and
for the accuracy of which the relieving officer is permanently responsible.

Let me briefly consider the heads of investigation I have
mentioned above.

1st. *The occupation.* The ordinary occupation of the
applicant should of course be given, and yet at many
Boards now this is only obtained accidentally, as it were,
by asking for it. It should form an item as a matter of
course in the statement of the case before the Guardians.

2nd. *The wages* earned when employed at the regular
occupation, and the earnings coming in at the time the
application for relief is made. These are most important
matters, and yet most difficult to get at. The statements
made by applicants are unfortunately rarely to be relied
upon, and often no definite information is formally given
by the relieving officer. The consequence is that most
Boards are constantly deceived, and know that they are so

deceived. Nobody ever makes out a proper statement; the applicants nearly all prevaricate, if they do not absolutely tell falsehoods, and relief is given in hundreds of cases on this unsatisfactory basis. The relieving officer should, even at the cost of time and labour, find out all about earnings past and present if it be possible for him to do so. In cases of fraud and deceit, or, whenever information is purposely kept back, out-door relief should be at once stopped.

3rd. *Previous relief.* This information is now never obtained. It is occasionally stated that such and such a case has been on the Parish very often, but no regular detailed information is put before the Board. It would be most important if it were supplied from books, such as those described at p. 171, which are kept by some branches of the Charity Organization Society, and found to be essential to the proper working of that Institution. Nothing, perhaps, can possibly give a better idea of a case than a history of its dealings with the Parish. A list or register or ledger, as it might be called, with an alphabetical index might easily be compiled from the books of the Union. From this all information concerning the previous relief of any pauper could be obtained with very little trouble and with only an expenditure of a few pounds in preparing and keeping up the books.

4th. *Members of Friendly Societies, Clubs, etc.* The question whether a man has belonged to a Friendly Society or has been thrifty in some way or other, is one of vital importance in considering his relief. I am aware that the law on this point is a great anomaly, but that we must nevertheless act according to its requirements. I maintain, however, that we should in the interest of the poor, and in the interest of the ratepayers be as considerate and liberal as possible to those, who, whether from protracted illness or from any other cause, are obliged to come to the Parish, but who have endeavoured as far as in them lay to provide for themselves, and who have made sacrifices while in work to prevent themselves from having to fall immediately on the Parish when overtaken by any continuous calamity which is in no way their fault or preventible by them. Further than this, this information would enable the Parish to be strict in refusing out-door relief to cases of persons who have been employed as railway servants, and in other situations where sick and such-like clubs exist and are readily available, but who have resolutely declined to become members. Such cases are most common, and should not be allowed out-door relief or even out-door Medical relief. They not only know the proper means of providing for themselves, but they have every facility for so doing at a trifling cost, and they must indeed really resist the better influence of their companions and brother workmen, by refusing to make use of these advantages.

5th. *Relations.* The question of the existence of relatives is one which is also much neglected because it is so troublesome, and it is so much easier to grant a little relief than to take the trouble of investigating a matter closely. The easier we make the obtaining of this relief, and the more readily we grant it to a case where there are relatives who should legally come forward, and who are in a position to do so, so much the more do we absolutely and directly loosen the family tie, and encourage the unnatural desire now so often to be met with, of avoiding the support of old parents and relations, and handing them over to the Parish. Boards should not grudge the spending of time and money in hunting up legally responsible relatives, even if the cost of so doing be greater than the amount of relief saved. The register referred to (p. 171), will be a great assistance in tracing these cases.

6th. *Criminal convictions.* The question of an applicant having been convicted is one which is but rarely considered. Many, indeed, think it is unfair to go into the matter. Of course I do not mean to say that one offence is to brand a person for ever; that one conviction for drunkenness, for example, is to be a bar to a man's being on the lists till the day of his death; but I do say that any one who has been recently convicted even of drunkenness is not a person to whom out-door relief should be allowed. Granting it, simply means that his earnings go to the publican, so that the taxes which his hard-working neighbour has to pay really encourage him in his craving for drink. Whenever a criminal conviction is noted against a man or woman additional care should be exercised, and there should always be some very alleviating circumstances before out-door relief is granted.

7th. *Illegitimate children.* As regards the parents of illegitimate children the greatest possible care should be taken. God forbid that we should wish to be hard upon any human being or to cast the first stone at a fallen sister, but as a matter of morality relief to those with illegitimate children should in almost all cases be confined to the Workhouse. Unless we do this we shall, as we are so apt to do by our present system, be really subsidizing the earnings of the prostitutes residing in the Union. As in the previous case a note in the register indicating this failing should involve extra care, and out-door relief should only be granted in very special and peculiarly alleviating circumstances (see also p. 82).

The main objections which will be raised against the proposal of such a rigid investigation as I have suggested, will be that the staff of relieving officers will not be able to undertake the duty. I dwell more particularly on the staff and duties of relieving officers in the next section of this chapter, but it may be as well to mention one or two points here.

As a rule, the staff of relieving officers does not increase with the population of paupers. In my Union, I found that in 1861 we had one relieving officer for every 16,832 inhabitants, and in 1873 one for every 18,750. These officers' districts also were necessarily unevenly divided, one containing no fewer than 21,368 inhabitants. It is simply impossible for the officers to do what is necessary over such large areas, and on this point I will quote from a letter from the Poor Law Inspector, Mr. Doyle, published in the second annual report of the Local Government Board, p. 66. After giving a list of districts, Mr. Doyle states as follows :—

"Looking to the acreage, population, pauperism and expenditure, in these several districts, it is impossible to avoid the conclusion that the duty imposed upon the officers is in the majority of cases so onerous that no man, however active and intelligent, can satisfactorily discharge them. There are, it is true, some districts in which the number of paupers under the charge of one relieving officer does not exceed 200, but there are others in which the number exceeds 1000. In a very large number of

cases it is considerably above 500. It is simply impossible
that a relieving officer can visit at reasonably short
intervals the several cases that are under his care, or that
he can make himself acquainted with the varying circumstances of them, and personally administer the relief that
has been ordered by the Guardians. I am sure that the
first step towards improving the administration of relief is
to reduce the relief districts, that no relieving officer shall
have under his charge a greater number of cases than it
will be possible for him to visit and thoroughly investigate
at least once in every quarter, in addition to visiting and
reporting upon every fresh application, after careful
inquiry into all the circumstances of each case. I am
bound to say that at present the information afforded by
the relieving officers is, comparatively speaking, of little
value. Rarely are they able to inform the Guardians of
the exact circumstances of the family and relations of
applicants for relief. It thus happens that a very large
number of persons are in receipt of parochial relief who
are not without resources, or who have relations able to
maintain them, but who are never called upon to do so."

Having considered this matter so far from a general-
policy point of view, the new Guardian will no doubt wish
to see its effect on the poor themselves. How then will
such a strict investigation as I propose affect the poor?
In the first place, who would fear it? Not the deserving.
Those whose cases would bear the closest investigation
would be only too glad to have them looked into, for they
would be more likely to receive liberal relief. Those who
are undeserving of consideration would, it is true, object
to it, and object to it strongly. They would know that

their past history and conduct would be examined into carefully and rigidly. They would know that in appealing to the relieving officer they would have to make a clean breast of it, for if they did not, and if they made any false statements, as they now so constantly do, and with such success, the careful investigation would find them out, and their dishonesty would, of course, go against them and make out-door relief hopeless. Further, would not this very consideration prevent many hundreds, and I may say thousands, from coming to the Parish at all? The habitual drunkard, the reckless and improvident would learn wisdom by such rules. The apparent harshness with such cases would be the true kindness. In a few years it would render many squalid homes happy, and many an improvident and miserable hovel the abode of comfort.

Another objection which the new Guardian will find raised against this proposal will be the time which the considering of such investigations will involve. For argument's sake, suppose this plan were at first to take longer than the haphazard system of little or no investigation ; this consideration is unimportant compared with the question of the efficient working of the relief. The Board can be split up into Relief Committees of from five to six members, who are amply sufficient to consider cases when a general policy has been adopted. As a matter of fact, however, it will soon appear the more carefully each case is attended to the less the week's work will ultimately become. I have already said that many cases now relieved and considered time after time would never think of applying at all under the proposed system of investigation, and that many hundreds of persons who now claim the Parish aid as a matter of course, would never venture near a relieving officer.

It would be found that the weekly work would be soon so reduced that the extra time which each case might take, though that would be materially lessened when all the facts were before the Board in writing, would be more than counterbalanced by the shortness of the list of applicants. If charity too were working in harmony with the Guardians (page 178), still more time would be saved, and still fewer cases would have to be gone into.

Another objection will be that much of the information which I urge should be given is already contained in the chairman's book, and that what is not there is stated verbally by the relieving officer. Some of the information no doubt is in this book, but not many of the most material points I have referred to, and besides, it should be before the members as well as the chairman. As regards the verbal statements of the relieving officer, these are, as I have before stated, not sufficient, and are very apt to be vague and general. They are altogether different from a written report of ascertained facts.

A mechanical difficulty may be suggested as to the copying out of these lists for the weekly meetings in those Unions where each Guardian is supplied with a list of applications, and where relief is granted by the whole Board and not by a committee. Of course if these lists contain so much information they will be longer and more difficult to copy; but such an objection is trivial, for the cost of printing, if it enabled the work to be done more efficiently, is not worth considering. A small lithographic

press, however, might be obtained, and by writing one copy
on transfer paper, plenty of the inmates of the Workhouse would be able in a week or two to use the stone
sufficiently well for the purpose of providing a couple of
dozen copies.

No doubt the work of rigid investigation could not be
carried out without an increase to the staff of relieving
officers. So far an extra expense would be a consequence.
How, however, would the reduced number of applicants
counterbalance this? To judge from the Atcham Union,
where a most efficient system of investigation and careful
relief has been in operation for years, this extra cost would
be made up over and over again, to say nothing of the
benefit to the community.

The population of Atcham in 1836 was 17,855, in 1870
it had increased to 19,314, yet the return of pauperism
had decreased as follows:

In 1836 the number receiving in-door relief was . . 196
The number receiving out-door relief was 1199

Total 1395

Cost £9800

In 1870 the number receiving in-door relief was . . 140
The number receiving out-door relief was 139

Total 293

Cost £4230

Reduction in in-door paupers 42, and in out-door
paupers 1102, and in cost £5570.

The average cost per head is much more than under the old system. This is a very important fact, for it means that when relief is given to any individual it is given much more liberally, for it is well ascertained that the case is a deserving one. The total cost, however, to the community by the reduced number of paupers is less than half.

Such a result could not, of course, be accomplished in a week, for it has taken forty years at Atcham, but it need not be so long before a sensible effect would be produced. Sir Baldwin Leyton, the son of the baronet who was really the moving spirit at Atcham, says, " Less than forty months might suffice to make a serious diminution in even the most pauperised Unions, but what makes the difficulty so great is the habit of the people promoted by the present fatuous administration, and the absence of men capable and willing to devote themselves to the work."

The saving of the rates, if every parish could follow Atcham's example, would be very great. It would amount to several pence in the pound in most places, no small relief to the now over-taxed tradesman and others. This, however, is the very least part of the benefit of the change involved in taking the trouble of investigating the circumstances of each applicant for relief. The reduction of the number of poor, the wiping out of two-thirds from the pauper roll is far more important in every sense, and eventually the greatest benefit to the over-taxed tradesman. The Guardian who can secure this change will confer an incalculable good on the Union to which he belongs, and to the country at large, of which he is a citizen.

(b) *The Staff of Relieving Officers.*

The new Guardian will soon perceive that almost the whole efficiency of the administration of relief depends upon the relieving officers. It is for this reason that they should be men of intelligence and education, and the salary given to them should not be such as to make it impossible for any but a broken-down publican, or failure in some other line of business, to accept the office. The duties are far from easy in themselves, and, what is more, they require tact and management which is not always or readily to be found. They also demand great firmness coupled with great kindness of manner, a determination to do work and to take trouble about matters which will make but little show, and which may often be shirked without any immediate consequence to the shirker. These are qualities which, when found, demand liberal remuneration, and no Union will be the poorer for obtaining the right class of men for its relieving officers, and for paying them on a generous scale.

The number of separate duties which devolve on these officers is larger than any one unacquainted with the subject might suppose, and the time which the performance of these duties must occupy is such as to render it imperative, if the work of the Union is to be done at all, for the staff to be sufficient. Nay, rather it is better and cheaper for this branch of the staff to be superabundant rather than too small. Among their regular duties I may mention the following :

1. The distribution of the relief granted by the Board. This alone is not a work to be speedily got through. In

the different districts into which most Unions are divided, there are usually a number of centres for the purpose of distribution; each of these must be visited at least once a week.

2. The visit to the schools and the looking-up of the school attendance, particularly in cases which the officer knows to be doubtful or irregular.

3. The investigation of new applications for relief, that is, a hunting-up of the circumstances and histories of the fresh cases who come each week before the Board. These require considerable time, judgment and skill. It often involves no small amount of travelling from one part of the Union to another, and even beyond the boundaries of the Union itself.

4. The making out of the various returns, clerical work, etc., and attending the weekly Board meetings.

5. The attending to accidental cases, which are always coming before the relieving officer in the discharge of his duties, and which demand immediate action.

6. The visiting of the permanent cases. There are in most Unions a large number of these whose names are on the annual revision lists (page 174). They mostly live in separate tenements, and, according to the Local Government Board, require to be visited at least once a quarter.

7. The in-door cases must also be watched. It may be said that the relieving officers have nothing to do with these, and this is true with some of them, but not so with many others. The only ones with whom they have nothing to do are the orphan children, all the other in-door paupers require to be more or less looked after. This is necessary for the purpose of seeing that relations do not

really exist who are legally bound to assist them, and that
persons are not permanently kept in the house who should
and could be maintained by relations.

These are some of the more obvious duties of relieving
officers, and, to enable a proper check to be kept, every
officer should be required to keep a journal showing the
exact visits made each day, and the exact mode in which
he has occupied his time. This plan is not often adopted,
though strongly recommended by the Local Government
Board. It is naturally resented by the officers, or rather
by those who are not heart and soul in their work. Without such a journal, however, it is impossible to get at exact
information as to the visits which have been made, or to be
satisfied that each officer really does his duty. The journals, which should be laid on the Board table each week,
will also help the Guardians materially in deciding whether
the staff is sufficient.

The new Guardian, looking at the work of the officer
from a common-sense point of view, and calculating the
actual number of hours which each of these main branches
of employment will occupy considering the size and population of his district, will often find that it is impossible for
him to do what he should, even by working regularly at
the highest pressure, a plan of work which as a constant
condition is most undesirable to require. The truth of the
matter is that at the present time many relieving officers
are not doing what they should, not from any fault of their
own, but from the fact that an impossible task is put on
them. Guardians, indeed, often shut their eyes to the fact
that the relieving officers are not looking into the cases
thoroughly. Things go on pretty well without it, anyhow

as well as they have done for years. Further than this they do not like the idea of adding to the staff because it looks like an increase to the expenditure. This notion is, as I have several times pointed out, quite fallacious, for an ample staff to investigate each case is the cheapest possible system. Any new Guardian, after having satisfied himself on this point, and found that his own Union is deficient, should lose no time in pointing it out, and urging that the staff of relieving officers be increased. He may do this on two grounds, firstly, on that of efficiency, and secondly, on that of absolute economy.

As regards efficiency. I presume it may be taken for granted as the most elementary axiom that it is necessary and desirable that the relieving officer should perform the duties which have been previously stated, and further, that he should do this thoroughly. This supposition is, indeed, the only justification for appointing relieving officers at all. Now, if this be the case, it will be simple to ascertain in any particular Union whether it is possible for the staff to get through the work during the working hours of the day. Let the new Guardian, if he really wishes to ascertain all about it, go with the officer for a few days and judge for himself ; it will be easy to see whether there are hours enough in the day for him to get through his work in a thoroughly efficient and satisfactory manner.

The length of the working week is as follows. Sundays must, of course, be omitted, though relieving officers may often be obliged to attend to urgent cases on that day. The greater part of another day is taken up with attending the Board of Guardians, so that but five clear days remain. The length of each day cannot be taken as more than nine hours. This is as much as can be reasonably expected from a relieving officer, particularly as he is liable at any moment, both day and night, to be called out on duty for sickness, etc.

If then in any Union the Guardian finds that there is absolutely not enough time for the actual performance of the duties, it must be obvious that some portions of the work are either left undone altogether or that they are all gone through in a most off-hand, perfunctory, and inefficient manner.

Let me now say a few words on the subject of the economy of an ample staff of relieving officers. As I pointed out in a former section of this chapter, the more searching the investigation of each case is made the more certain it is that the habitual vagabond and the thriftless impostor will be sifted out of the pauper roll, or only relieved within the walls of the Workhouse. Directly the investigation is relaxed so surely will it be found that the lists of applicants become longer, that the relief will get more sought after, and the demoralisation of the people will increase.

At the lowest the average relief granted per case is 2s. 6d. and three loaves for four weeks, or say 16s. a case. If then each extra relieving officer were paid £150 a year, and this is a very much larger salary than is generally given, and he prevented only four improper cases a week coming in for relief, his salary would be more than covered. At how many Boards of Guardians could it be asserted that not four cases a week are hastily decided without proper and ample investigation?

This consideration was very singularly confirmed in my

own Union. In 1872 one of the districts was divided in half, and an additional relieving officer appointed. In 1873, although it so happened that fifty-three weeks' relief were included in it as compared with fifty-two in 1872, the total out-door relief was reduced by £432, or nearly 12 per cent. If the fifty-third week had not been considered £62 more would have been deducted, for that was the average relief each week, making the saving just £500, or more than 13 per cent. The unfortunate officer was only paid £80 a year, so that the saving amounted to nearly seven times his salary. A slight part of the reduction may have happened from natural causes, but no doubt the main result was due almost entirely to his appointment, and to the beneficial effect of a more complete and rigid investigation of the circumstances of each applicant, a looking after each case, in fact, in a way which it was impossible could be done when the two districts were under one relieving officer. This view of the facts was proved further by the pauperism in the other districts of the same Union, where no addition had been made to the relieving officer's staff, having decreased during the same period by a very small and almost an inappreciable amount only.

The direct saving then in money in this instance, by this judicious step, was considerable, but the benefit to the people was immensely more. Every one who is kept off the rates not only represents so many shillings saved to the ratepayers, but is one more centre of honourable independence, one more working bee instead of one more drone, one more useful citizen instead of one more drag and burden.

The absolute staff of relieving officers, must to a certain

extent depend on the extent and nature of the Union, but as a general rule that given by Mr. Doyle (page 157) is a fair average one. This states that 500 is quite the outside number of paupers which any relieving officer should be required to look after. The new Guardian should, therefore, endeavour to induce his Board to adopt this scale and to regard this number of paupers to each relieving officer quite as the maximum. Not only, be it remembered, is it necessary to have an ample staff during the light season of the year, but it is wiser and, as I have endeavoured to show, cheaper for the staff to be always ready to cope with the work even in the heaviest time of the year. Efficient relieving officers, it must be remembered, cannot be obtained at a moment's notice, or ordered, like so much merchandize, just as required.

(c) *Relieving Officers Holding other Appointments.*

After what has been stated as to the duties of the relieving officers and the length of time which their necessary and ordinary routine of work involves, it will not be wondered at that I should urge on all Guardians not to allow their relieving officers to hold any other appointments. It is true that this rule is adopted in the regulations which are issued for the guidance of Guardians, which state in Article 164 as follows:—

"No person shall hold the office of relieving officer "unless he be able to keep accounts, and unless "he reside in the district for which he may be ap- "pointed to act, devote his whole time to the per- "formance of the duties of his office and abstain from

" following any trade or profession, and from entering into
" any other service."

This clause is however followed by another by which
the Guardians are empowered to dispense with it, provided
the consent of the Local Government Board be previously
obtained. In this, as in most of the provisions of the Poor
Law, absolute power seems vested in the Local Government
Board. It must be obvious, however, that this second rule
is only intended to be applied in very small places, and
especially in agricultural districts where many relieving
officers act as registrars of Births and Deaths. In such
places there may be advantages in a man like the relieving
officer who is about the country regularly looking after this
work, and it may be difficult to get any one else to do it at
a reasonable rate. In towns and other districts, however,
this is not necessary, and it is much to be objected to. I
have seen large Unions where it has been allowed by the
Local Government Board, much to the detriment of the
Poor Law work. In one case I know a relieving officer
with a district of over 22,000 inhabitants, covering
fourteen square miles, who also acts as registrar for this
large area. He must make indeed a larger income by his
extra employment than by his original office.

When men have been appointed and their appointment
has been approved by the Local Government Board,
no Board of Guardians has power to remove them or to
alter the arrangement, except with the further sanction of
the Local Government Board. Consequently a Guardian
will find it difficult to change an arrangement which has
existed for some time. The relieving officer will not care
to have his earnings reduced, and the Local Government

Board after having given their sanction will not readily reverse their previous decision, and without this the officer cannot be compelled to give up his additional appointment, however much the district may have enlarged or otherwise changed. It is very important, therefore, in new appointments to consider these matters, and especially to oppose the introduction of any precedent which may lead to the relieving officers considering themselves allowed to devote their time and attention to any duties but those connected with their office. Of course it follows if this be done that the remuneration given must be liberal, and the salary allowed to the officers must not be so small as to give them a fair excuse for trying to add to their means of living.

(d) *Book of the History of each Case.*

A want which the new Guardian will much feel with reference to the investigation of cases will be some authentic and readily accessible account of each, its Parish history, in fact, arranged as it were in a sort of ledger, each individual having one or more folios according to its dealings with the establishment. In the first section of this chapter I dwelt on the importance of some such definite history of the Parish dealings of each individual. This plan has been adopted on a small scale by some of the branches of the Charity Organisation Society, and a wonderfully useful work they find it to be. In fact it has become almost essential to the efficient conduct of their operations.

In order to get some idea of what such a book would

reveal, I prepared a small one for one Parish in my own Union, and extracted all the relief given to each person in that Parish during the previous ten years. The Parish formed an agricultural village not giving one the impression of poverty like the low parts of some towns, but any one driving through it would say it had the appearance of a well-to-do place in every sense of the word, and it was situated within nine miles of London. I only selected it because its size enabled me to do what I wished. It was large enough for my purpose, and not too populous to occupy too much of my time. I think ten years may be taken as a very short period for the average residence of each inhabitant in an agricultural place; I should say that fifteen years was nearer the mark, but I took ten years only, and I found that in this Parish with an average of 550 inhabitants no fewer than 124 separate adults and 143 separate children had been relieved during the ten years. This gave a total of 267 individuals relieved, or as nearly as possible one half the population.

Some of the cases thus placed side by side in alphabetical order were most instructive. The same family name came over and over again. Of one family I found no fewer than thirteen had been relieved during the ten years.

First came the great-grandmother, who died at 90 years of age; then came her numerous family—James, Edward, Elizabeth, Richard, Samuel and Maria, each one on and off the Parish during the whole period, and all but two having had out-door relief. Then came the grandchildren and great-grandchildren, some beginning at five years of age to get a share, four of them obtaining an outfit of clothes. In short, the history revealed the fact that this prolific grandmother had permanently produced a plentiful family of paupers coming to the Parish on every emergency.

A book such as this small specimen, made to include the whole Union, would be an invaluable assistance in deciding on cases as they came up. It would contain all the points of information referred to at page 152, and as much more as might be necessary, in the curtest form. The dates of each application, the amounts granted, the refusals to grant relief, and so forth, would all be included. The refusals would be particularly important, as this would prevent that changing of decision which is so objectionable and to which special reference is made at page 87. An alphabetical index would enable each person's history to be found in a moment, and every point would get noted down either for or against, so as to secure a thorough knowledge of the circumstances without which it is impossible to relieve judiciously.

It will be said that such a work would be very large, that it would fill many volumes and be an expensive thing to compile and keep up. No doubt it would, in the extensive Unions especially, but its cost would be amply repaid in securing a complete knowledge of facts, and by the saving of time in placing them before the Board. In very large Unions it might be well to begin with a volume for each letter of the alphabet, with an index to each volume. These would be kept in the Board Room, ready to be referred to, and posted up from week to week. The labour of preparing the books in the first instance would be considerable, but a quick clerk would do a great deal in a few months. Probably it would be sufficient to go back only for 10 years.

Possibly there are but few Boards of Guardians who would at once agree to the preparation of such a history of the cases, and even when they were willing it would be necessary in the first instance to apply to the Local Government Board for permission to expend money for the purpose. When completed, however, it would not only be of the most every-day use, but it would throw much light on the subject of pauperism. It would show conclusively the ingredients of which the present pauper roll is made up, and it would also indicate how it is added to, whether or no the great mass of pauperism is hereditary or whether it is largely added to each year by cases of unavoidable misfortune.

I would strongly urge on all new Guardians to consider this subject, and endeavour to get it carried out. As a test of its use, let them themselves prepare a portion of such a return, say a list of all the paupers relieved during five or ten years, whose names begin with the letter A. This any one can do, from the printed lists published half-yearly or from the relief books. I feel sure that this specimen will convince most of the use the complete books would be, and make them use their endeavours to secure their preparation in each Union.

(e) *Annual Revision of Permanent Cases.*

A custom exists in many Unions of having an annual revision of the so-called permanent cases. This annual list tends to become very long, and it is the aim of all paupers who know what they are about, to try and get on to it.

It is supposed to contain all those persons who are so old or so afflicted, as to render it practically certain that they will receive out-door relief all their lives. It is true that the law does not recognise permanent out-door relief, and that the regulations require that all cases should be gone into periodically and reconsidered by the Guardians. The fact, however, of a case only coming up once a year tends to make the relief almost the same thing as a permanent annuity.

When the annual revision time comes round, however, it is invariably found that a few of those who have been so comfortably receiving relief, are not really entitled to it at all—some hidden resource comes to light, some private store is discovered, which really renders the recipient quite above needing the Parish dole, although he may have been receiving it for years. I have known such a Parish pensioner turn out to possess two or three houses or cottages of his own.

The way these annual revisions take place in some Unions is as follows. The number of paupers to be seen is too great to be taken at the ordinary meeting, so that three or four extra special meetings are held. Sometimes these assemble in different parts of the Union. On the days fixed a few only of the Guardians attend, usually those who represent the special Parishes to be taken on the day, but of course any Guardian is at liberty to come if he thinks proper to do so. The permanent cases present themselves in hundreds, and the relief is in the majority of cases renewed until the next revision, that is, for another year. Some, as I have said, from some cause or other coming to light for the first time,

are struck off the list. At the beginning of the day a
minute or two is taken with each case, but as the
time goes and the long list remains to be finished
the paupers are usually settled off with remarkable
celerity.

Nothing perhaps tends to promote imposition more
than this annual revision, and it is quite unnecessary,
if a Board of Guardians really work efficiently. When a
case is settled for a year, and relief given "till the
next revision," the chances are ten to one that the
relieving officer never goes near it till just before that next
revision, that is, when he knows it must again come up
before the Board. He should of course visit all permanent
cases at least every three months; but this is expecting
too much from a man whose district is probably so large
that, slave as he will, he can hardly keep up with current
work.

In a small Union there can be no possible reason for
this annual revision, and in a large Union it can be quite
well dispensed with, if the Board of Guardians will only
form two, three, or more relief committees, composed of
say five members each. All cases should then, be they
permanent or not, be brought before the Board at least
once every three months, with a report from the relieving officer of his visit. With the book of the history of
each pauper (p. 171) these cases would take very little
time; but any change in their circumstances, or anything
which might influence the Guardians in their grant, either
to make it more or less, would not fail to be brought before
them.

I would strongly urge on all new Guardians the desirability of trying to do away with this system of annual revision, and to require all cases to come up in their ordinary course at the Board Meetings at least once every three months.

CHAPTER XXIX.

THÉ HARMONIOUS CO-OPERATION BETWEEN CHARITY AND LEGAL RELIEF.

HE absolute importance in every Union of the harmony and systematic mutual working between Charitable relief and Poor Law relief, if the utmost amount of good is to be secured, is so obvious that it may seem unnecessary for me to enter into the subject argumentatively. Obvious as it is, however, there are but very few Unions which act on this principle, nay, I know of no one which does so to the fullest extent, and the new Guardian will find it one of his most difficult tasks to secure its proper adoption. The obstacles which beset the carrying out of this co-operation do not rest only with the Guardians themselves, but they have to be overcome also on the part of the clergy and others who represent the charity of the district. Not a few regard the Guardians as essentially hard and cruel, and the very notion of any co-operation with themselves they look upon instinctively as they would that of an attempt to mingle oil with water. This feeling is, it is true,

in some places being got over, thanks in no small degree
to the admirable work of the Charity Organisation Society
and the extension of the Poor Law Guardian Conferences.
It will, however, in most districts, require great patience
and perseverance on the part of the new Guardian before
he can succeed in carrying out this reform, essential
though it be to the proper administration of the Poor
Law and the wise and beneficial Charitable relief of the
poor.

Looking at the matter of relief from the lowest point
of view, and simply considering that the cost comes out of
the pockets of all ratepayers, many of whom are not much
removed from the pauper class itself, the Guardians in
granting relief are bound to be influenced to a very great
extent by the charitable assistance which is obtained by
each individual from private sources. Parish relief is
after all only to be the last resource ; it is only to be sufficient to supply the absolute and essential wants of the
applicant ; and one element of consideration in judging of
each case, and of granting it aid, should be a knowledge
of how far the private sources which are at work also,
relieving and assisting suffering and distress, have been
exercised in that particular case. Without this, vast sums
of public rates may be and indeed often are devoted to
those who are amply provided for by kind and charitable
friends.

Leaving this first and obvious consideration, and going
deeper and regarding all relief and charitable agency as
working for the permanent benefit of the community, the
co-operation between these organs becomes more important even than before. The two organisations of relief

N 2

should be indeed as it were twin sisters, and should act as completely in union with one another as twin sisters generally are supposed to do. Without this action the greatest amount of good cannot be done either by the Guardians on the one hand, or by the clergy, ministers, and other charitable agencies on the other.

The first step to bring about this most desirable result should, however, not come from the Guardians but from the charitable agencies in the district. It will be obvious that the Guardians cannot co-operate to advantage with charity unless charity has already co-operated with herself. If a thousand and one agencies exist in a district for charitable relief, all or many of them competing with one another, as it were, and relieving the same persons half-a-dozen times over, the co-operation between one of them and the Poor Law though desirable is yet but a very small advance. The bringing of these Charitable agencies together, or as many as may be, will be the first task of the new Guardian, and this he will have to do, of course, in his private capacity. He should speak to the most influental of each of the leading bodies; if he is himself a leading man in any of them, this will help materially. He must, however, not expect to succeed at once; but if he persist in his endeavours, the benefits when once stated and argued about are so obvious to all who really mean to act in the best way they can for their fellow-creatures, that in the long-run he cannot fail to secure his object. He will gradually educate the party, and in time bring about some sort of co-operation among the charitable agencies, possibly imperfect at first, but quite sufficient to begin the reform upon.

Considering the size of most Unions, considering the number of clergy and ministers of all denominations who are at work in them, and considering the complete system of organisation which fraud, professional begging, and itinerant mendicancy has established, it is indeed strange that those who have been so long at work trying to secure the most good to the deserving, and to prevent the undeserving, the idle, and the profligate, from making a harvest at the expense of the diligent, have not long ago had a counter-organisation whereby, without considering trouble, expense, or pains, the case of every applicant for alms might be sifted to the very bottom. Such an organisation would be able, after full inquiry, to help with the liberal hand of charity all deserving cases, to support a tottering brother or sister at all hazards, and to prevent him from falling. It would also on the other hand be able firmly to hand over every case of fraud, regular beggary, or imposition of any sort, to the Guardians, to deal with according to the law, namely, simply to give such food and shelter as might be essential for bodily health within the walls of the Union House.

Should the new Guardian succeed in inducing some of the leading charitable agencies to combine and co-operate together for the common good, and form a charity committee, his next task will be to induce his brother Guardians also to work in harmony with this organization. This again will not be done in a moment, and the chances are, it will require considerable patience. The step will be very much hastened, however, and everything will be greatly facilitated if the Board consists of gentlemen of position, and those who are also interested in the charities of the district. Some of the more obvious results of this co-operation will be as follows :—

1. The aiding by private charity those about to apply for the Parish relief for the *first* time either in consequence of illness or some other misfortune, and the establishment of a charitable agency for examining into such cases. When found to be deserving, and when the aid is likely to be of *permanent* benefit, the assisting of this class by *temporary* charity, chiefly by means of loans. In this way many may be saved from the demoralizing effect of coming on the Parish and becoming paupers.

2. The complete knowledge which the organisation would obtain of each case, and of its resources, and the consequent prevention of a duplication of the relief, to any particular individual, either from the numerous charitable agencies or from the Poor Law.

3. The prevention of hardship to the deserving; for the Charity Committee would make it its business to investigate in time all the out-door cases, and itself aid any case, where a temporary assistance on a more liberal scale of gift, or loan, than the parish allowance, would be a permanent benefit.

4. The prevention of fraud by the undeserving, for the Parish could, without hesitation, give the Workhouse and the Workhouse only to those whom the Charity Committee reported as undeserving, and who from indolence or other causes endeavoured to inflict themselves on the bounty of the benevolent.

5. The careful assistance of widows, the facilitating of their removal to places where they could earn an independent livelihood (p. 52). The promotion of Provident Dis-

pensaries (see p. 46). The rescuing of casuals (see p. 72), and the management and rescue of young girls with illegitimate children (see p. 82).

6. Generally, as is over and over again dwelt upon in these pages, the prevention of persons from falling on the Parish, and the rescuing of those who really mean to improve, though they may have already fallen.

It must be evident that one of the most important ways of reducing the pauperism of any Union is the cutting off of *new* applicants. If we could accomplish this altogether for a few years, we should soon have very little to do in the way of relief. This is the reason why I lay so much stress, in another place, on the management of the children. At present, however, besides the young we continually add to our list week after week, and it is here that this Organised Charity acting in co-operation with the Parish could do so much. The causes which are at work in leading persons to come to the Parish for the first time may broadly be divided into three classes :—

1. Old age and permanent infirmity.
2. Temporary trouble.
3. Temporary sickness.

Concerning the old and infirm, if they have spent good and useful lives, they should rather be kept altogether by private alms and Christian charity, of which there is a constant supply for all good purposes, than by the dole of Parish relief. I believe that such an organisation of charity would tend to this, and a great blessing it would be to the poor as well as to those who give. This, however, is not one of the most important considerations, for we may hope that in time, by a wise administration of relief

and charity, and a promotion of thrift, the number of old
who have to depend during the end of their days on relief
will be reduced to a minimum, and will contain within its
number but few if any deserving cases.

It is for those who are still young, and who are struck
down by some temporary trouble, that the greatest amount
of good is to be done. These, it seems to me, are now but
too frequently being made into permanent paupers instead,
as so many might be, of being rescued by the timely and
liberal hand of charity. When such cases come before a
Board of Guardians, they receive the dole of a few
shillings a week and some loaves; they are dragged to
the Union House, the very name of which is degrading to
an honourable spirit; they become associated with the
Workhouse and Parish relief, and familiarized with the idea
of pauperism. A man will think long before he comes to
the Parish for the *first* time, but he comes more readily the
second, when the ice is once broken, and he is apt soon to
begin to prefer getting for nothing what he can only earn
by toil elsewhere. He gradually looks upon the Parish as
his natural provider, and, in but too many cases, in a short
time, his honourable independence is gone, and he, his
wife, and his children gradually sink down into chronic
paupers.

The Organization of Charity working with the Parish and
in harmony with its relieving officers, would change this.
Such cases, if discovered by the relieving officer, would be
seized by the tender but wise hands of charity. New cases
would be looked upon as suitable for charity, if they could
stand *a careful and rigid investigation*, and if necessary, a
liberal help in the shape of a loan or otherwise might put

many on their feet and rescue them and their family from the arms of the Parish altogether. Who amongst the well-to-do classes has not at one time or another in his experience had to thank some friend for a lift up out of some trouble? This is exactly what a poor man at times requires, and what charity should delight to give with no grudging hand, but what the Parish relief money can never be made to do.

One opposition to this proposal which the new Guardian will be sure to have to refute, will be the extra trouble it will involve on the Board. This is altogether a mistake, for it will tend vastly to reduce the work at the Board, and, what is far more important, it will lead to a reduction of the number on the relief list. I do not hesitate to say such a system will very soon and very materially reduce the pauper roll of any parish. As a corollary, it will in the next place reduce the rates, which in most Unions are high and oppressive, not so much perhaps to the well-to-do as to those who, by hard and honourable labour, with difficulty keep themselves above the level of the paupers they relieve. Moreover, it will promote the improvement of all classes, and it will enable that large number of persons who are only too anxious to do what good they can, to do real good, not merely to give their money indolently and carelessly, but it will afford them a means of *preventing* poverty rather than simply relieving it when it has worked its mischief.

When the new Guardian has succeeded both in inducing the clergy to co-operate together, and the Guardians to work in harmony with the charitable committee thus formed, it will be well to have a meeting of all those who are interested in the movement, and even to repeat this yearly or at some other fixed period. The chairman of the Board of Guardians should preside, and all the clergy, ministers, and others, whether they have yet joined or no, should be asked to attend. Such a conference well managed may do immense good, and promote the object to a great extent, and keep the interest of the inhabitants in the movement. The experiences and difficulties would be discussed, and arrangements mutually made at such conferences for the better and more efficient working of the district. I sincerely hope that some day we may see such an organization of charity working in every Union hand in hand and side by side with each Poor-Law machinery. When this has been accomplished, we shall hear very little more of deserving persons starving, or begging vagabonds thriving. Charity and relief will work together for the good of all, the former will heap blessings on the deserving and give them a chance of rescuing themselves from misfortune, and the latter will reserve its stern assistance within the walls of the Workhouse to the professional beggar, the impostor, the improvident, and the reckless.

CHAPTER XXX.

RELIEF ON LOAN.

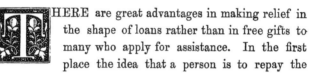HERE are great advantages in making relief in the shape of loans rather than in free gifts to many who apply for assistance. In the first place the idea that a person is to repay the amount of aid prevents its being as demoralizing as it would be if the same relief were absolutely given. A person of good feeling would much prefer repaying what was granted to him; and though the obligation is still great, it is not nearly so humiliating as the asking for and acceptance of the Parish gift. In the second place, and what is perhaps more important, the repayment is a direct encouragement to thrift. The person in repaying the loan soon sees the importance of regular though only of small savings, and the very collection of the loan may be the means of inducing many to continue the act of saving on their own account after the loan has been repaid. Besides this, these persons are very sharp, and if they *know* they will be required to repay they will think more than once before they incur the liability of asking for relief.

From the ratepayers' point of view the greater fairness of loans to all who can by an effort repay them is obvious. Many ratepayers there are who would be very glad of a little relief themselves at times if they could get it, and find it no easy matter to pay their rates. It is extremely unfair to tax such as these for the free relief of those who could, by a little less self-indulgence when in health and full work, repay the assistance they so readily ask for on the least pretext.

There are two classes who would be chiefly affected by a system of loans and these are:—

1st. The able-bodied in temporary distress from some sudden misfortune, as the want of work, a death in the family and the consequent expense of burial, or from requiring to purchase some costly surgical instrument.

2nd. The able-bodied man's family applying for temporary relief on account of the illness of the chief bread-winner, including also the doctor's fee and the special medical materials supplied.

Few will dispute that the first class should as far as possible be prevented from coming to the Parish at all, and that if they do come it would be far better to let them have the temporary relief, if given out of the Workhouse, by way of loan rather than as a free gift. In many places indeed some attempt is made in this direction, and occasionally relief is nominally granted on loan to these cases.

The second category, however, is very rarely so treated, and this is by far the more important of the two.

Any one attending at a Board of Guardians, and

particularly the new member, will be struck with the number of cases of relief which are passed as a matter of course by the relieving officer merely saying, "Medical relief." "Illness of the man." "Illness of the woman." (see chapter 8). There is rarely a question, and scarcely any consideration of the circumstances, and illness is without doubt the great portal through which recruits for the pauper ranks throughout the country are continually passing. Some of these cases are no doubt old and permanently disabled, but a large number of the majority are able-bodied persons in temporary illness. Why should these become paupers? Why do they not belong to Medical Dispensaries, Friendly Societies, and so forth? The answer is obvious. Those who are quite young men have been too heedless to think of illness, and it has come upon them unawares. Those who are older but still young and hearty "don't hold to clubs," as they so often say. They know full well the Parish is the best club for them. They pay in nothing and they draw out the full allowance. They soon get over any remnant of bashfulness in asking for the pauper's pittance. They soon learn to say to themselves, are not the rich made to pay the rates for us? why should we save the ratepayers by ourselves paying for what the rates are bound to supply us with for nothing?

What effect would a system of loans have on such as these? Would it not tend to make them provide for themselves and join clubs or some other independent and honourable society for promoting self-reliance? They would have no inducement then to depend on the Parish as they now have. The young and heedless would soon

see what was their interest, and even the older ones though
more difficult to impress would, after much grumbling, no
doubt, in time give up asking for Parish relief. They
would know that any relief they might get would have to
be repaid, and very soon they would find it cheaper to
insure against the consequences of illness by belonging to
some club or other independent society of their own,
rather than having anything to do with the relieving
officer.

As regards the repayments, there is no doubt but that they
must be rigidly enforced. It is no use making the loan a
mere farce. The instalments may be made in the first
instance light and easy, but they must be paid, and steps
must be taken if necessary to require regular repayment.
The experience of those who have made loans fully proves
that they are a great success if properly and firmly
managed. The Charity Organization Society has shown
this in many ways. Several Unions have proved it also,
and even charities have shown the advantages of the
system. Lord Shaftesbury's fund for aiding persons to
buy trucks, coffee-stalls, etc., has been worked on this plan
with immense success, and little if any difficulty has been
found in securing the payment of the instalments of the
loans. I am convinced that if a great many of the
so-called charities were conducted on a sort of loan
system, immense benefit would ensue to the recipients.

In some few cases no doubt, however firm and careful
the Collector, there might be a little difficulty in getting
the loans repaid. It might be necessary perhaps at times
to summon a defaulting creditor. Even this might not
secure repayment with a few very reckless individuals. In

such cases, however, on a second application for Parish
relief, which would be sure to come before long from the
same person, the Board finding the fact of the failure,
without special reason, to repay the first loan recorded in
the register (see p. 171) would have without any further
consideration to refuse all out-door assistance and to
decline to grant anything but the House. One or two
examples of this kind would practically secure the repayment of all loans, and in a very short time reduce the
number of applicants for relief.

The amount of payment as remuneration to the
Collector of such loans is a matter for consideration for
each Board. In all cases he must be paid by a commission
on the money he takes, and so obvious are the advantages
of the re-payment of the loans that it would conduce to the
benefit of the Union if, instead of *giving* the relief, the
Collector were allowed a hundred per cent. on the amount
he collected. To make his work remunerative he should
certainly receive 20 per cent., as it must be remembered
that the repayment will all be in small sums. He will
rarely receive more than a shilling from any place at which
he calls, he will consequently have to make a great many
visits before he collects a sovereign.

The question of the legality of loans must be mentioned,
and on this point I can refer to a correspondence I had
with the Local Goverment Board. It appears that under
article 4, No. 1, of the General Order of 7th October, 1865,
it is not legal for a relieving officer to act as Collector, but
a Collector must be a "special and separate officer."
Probably this is advisable, for there are obvious objections
to the person who gives relief being placed in the position

of a " Collector," and having perhaps at times to enforce repayment before a Court of Law. The granting of relief on loan is legal under article nine of the General Out-door Relief Regulation Order of the 14th December, 1852, but it must be borne in mind that it is necessary to declare at the time the relief is granted that it is given on loan. As regards the granting in the shape of a loan to be afterwards repaid, of all medical and other out-door relief to able-bodied persons during illness, the law only allows the actual cost incurred in the relief to be recovered. This makes it difficult to include the doctor's remuneration which is almost always by salary, so that unless the arrangement given on page 50 is adopted, it is advisable for the loan to be confined to the relief (including of course both money and kind) which is granted to the pauper.

The great difficulty in but too many cases of inducing a system of loans to be introduced, is the fact that gifts are so much easier and involve so much less trouble. The case is done with, and no more remains to be looked after when the relief is given, whereas a loan is a weekly trouble for months after the relief has ended. Besides this, the enforcing of repayment is not at all a grateful task. In spite of this, however, I would urge all new Guardians to take this matter up as soon as possible. Without question relief on loan in medical and other cases I have given, if enforced, tenderly though firmly for a year, would in the most remarkable way reduce the weekly list of applicants for Parish relief, and that too by inducing them to depend on their own efforts rather than on the Parish doles.

PART VI.

MISCELLANEOUS.

CHAPTER XXXI.

Ex-officio guardians.

THE law has provided that in every Union the Board of Guardians shall be composed of two classes: firstly, Guardians elected annually by the ratepayers, and, secondly, Guardians holding the office by virtue of their being magistrates residing in the Union. These last are called ex-officio Guardians. Generally, the number of ex-officio members of a Board is less than that of the elected Guardians, but they are usually sufficiently numerous to have considerable influence on the Boards, if they think proper to exercise it.

It is, perhaps, somewhat dangerous to speculate as to what were the intentions of the Legislature in making such a class as that of ex-officio Guardians. It seems, however, almost obvious that they were intended to be a sort of check in case of need to any popular feeling likely to influence prejudicially the working of the Poor Law, to act in fact as a sort of House of Lords, so as to be able to come to a calm decision on any matter without the fear of the loss of their seats influencing their opinion. As a rule also, they are men of higher social standing than the elected Guardians, and, what is more, they are usually from a better educated class.

It is obvious, however, that from whatever motive these ex-officio members of Boards of Guardians have been created, it was the intention that they should act at the meetings, and that the Boards to which they belong should at all events occasionally have the benefit of their attendance whenever any matter of unusual importance was under consideration. The desirability of their presence is clear. They are accustomed from the position they hold as magistrates, to take an impartial view of circumstances, and in considering even the ordinary relief cases, their time would occasionally be usefully engaged. No doubt it would be unreasonable to expect them all to attend every week. Their other duties occupy them a good deal, and generally they are men upon whose time much demand is made Each ex-officio Guardian, however, one might suppose could make a point of being present at least once or twice during the year, as well as on special occasions when important and unusual business is announced.

What, however, is the general rule concerning their attendance? Almost invariably ex-officio Guardians are noticeable only by their absence. On one Board I may mention with thirteen ex-officio Guardians, during a whole year only two ever presented themselves; one of these came but once, and the other three times. The year was remarkable for a Government inquiry into the over-crowding and imperfect state of the Workhouse, for a decision after a long fought controversy, to build new schools and new wings to the House, and for almost all the important points of Poor Law administration being under discussion. Had the ex-officio members been present, and entered into the various matters, their influence might have been most useful, and they would have been carrying out, one would suppose, the object for which their office was created.

I fear that this absence of the ex-officio Guardians is very common. The magistrates do not usually like the work of the Poor Law, but what is perhaps more the cause, they do not care to mix with the elected Guardians. When the elected Guardians are not exactly the sort of persons whom the ex-officio members care to associate with as equals, and to work with, the latter generally settle the difficulty by absenting themselves altogether from their meetings. They often say as a sort of excuse for not coming that the debates are so personal, the conduct is so strange, and the whole mode of procedure so contrary to their notions of what it should be, that they prefer not to go at all. Nothing can be a greater mistake than this. All these reasons so far from justifying absence, render their presence doubly important. If everything always went on right, there might be some excuse for their staying away. If, however, they openly acknowledge that things are not done as they should be, there is every reason for those coming, and coming regularly, who think so, and who can and have the independent position to say what they feel and think without caring for consequences. This is the only way the evils are ever likely to be remedied.

One of the most obvious reforms wanted in very many Unions is for a better and more educated class to become interested in the Local Government, and particularly in the administration of the Poor Law. Few duties require better men, for indeed the complicated questions which have to be settled, and the large influence for good or evil which Guardians exercise, might well make the best men hesitate in accepting the office. If ex-officio Guardians then thought proper to attend, and attend regularly, their presence would powerfully and rapidly induce leisure men of good standing in the different parishes to come forward as candidates for seats on the Board. Apart, then, from their direct influence in voting as Guardians, these ex-officio members have it in their power vastly and permanently to raise the standard of elected poor Law Guardians, and thus to promote the improved administration of relief.

The new Guardian should do his utmost with all the ex-officio members of his acquaintance to induce them to attend the meetings of the Board as often as may be. He will have some difficulty no doubt in doing this, but the greater the difficulty, the greater he may be sure will be the importance of his succeeding. The objections raised by the ex-officio Guardians may be turned into conclusive arguments why they should consider it their duty to attend the Board meetings. All who regard the poor and the Union as the important objects for which the Poor Law is established, must agree in the wisdom of having ex-officio Guardians, provided they will only do their duty. The good their presence may do at the meetings of the Boards, particularly in those places where it is least agreeable for them to attend, should induce these gentlemen as a body to take their seats at the weekly meetings for the administration of the Poor Law far more regularly than they now do.

CHAPTER XXXII.

WOMEN AS GUARDIANS OF THE POOR.

N these days, when so much is written and spoken of as to the duties and rights of women, it is somewhat difficult to suggest any change in existing customs without laying oneself open to the charge of advocating extreme opinions. At the same time I must add a few paragraphs in order to urge the importance of at least one or two women being members of every Board of Guardians. Strange as it may seem, there never appears to have been any legal restriction against women becoming candidates, although up to this day the number of Boards where they have seats is very few indeed. In some out of the way country districts, possibly women may be found holding this position, but in the larger towns it is very rare, and in London, as far as I can ascertain the first instance of an elected female Guardian was in 1875, when Mrs. Merington was returned for the Kensington Union.

There are many reasons why women should hold some position on each Board. In the first place, fully half the paupers are of their own sex, and although I do not lay much stress on this from a notion that men will not be equally fair to them, or that it requires a woman to secure impartiality in their treatment, yet I do think that good will in every way follow from a woman's eye and a woman's heart having an influence in the consideration of many of the cases which will weekly come before the Board. In the administration of the Workhouse, the Infirmary, the Schools both for boys, girls, and infants, it is obvious that a woman, even if she be in intelligence and education but up to the average standard of a Guardian, can inspect many details, and quickly see many defects which a body of men might overlook for years. In my own Workhouse, where seventeen infants did not go outside the walls for nine months ending August, such an event could not have happened if a woman had been in the habit of inspecting the House in the capacity of a Guardian.

In many Workhouses no woman ever crosses the door except she be a pauper, the matron, or a paid nurse. The matron may be an excellent person, but yet from her being always in the Workhouse, her ideas must of necessity become limited, and familiarity with pauperism and misery must almost of necessity affect her, and render her unfit to be the sole woman superintendent in her large household. The paid nurses also, however kind and good, require to be looked after in a way which no body of men Guardians can pretend to do.

Again, regarding the economy of the Workhouse, merely from the material point of view, a woman's notion of how the details should be managed is certainly far more likely to be practical than that of a man. As a matter of fact, at the present time these details are entirely in the hands of the Master and Matron. No doubt it is as well that this should be left so, and that these officers should be made responsible and held to be responsible. At the same time, however, it is highly desirable, if not absolutely essential, that every one connected with a Workhouse should know, as they do in almost every other institution, that their domestic doings and arrangements are under the eye of those who understand them, and who from their own knowledge are able to detect at once when and where anything goes wrong.

As regards out-door paupers, women Guardians may be invaluable, particularly those who have leisure and who are really intelligent persons. They can visit many cases of sickness, and gain an entrance, when men of necessity can do really nothing. I do not mean to say that Guardians or even women Guardians should become amateur relieving officers, but still there are many cases where a woman might elicit information and find out much concerning a case of distress, particularly with deserving people, which no man could possibly hope to do.

Women could also materially assist in promoting the co-operation between charity and the Poor Law. As a rule, those women who would be elected are just the persons who have to do with the charities of the district; and though it is probable that some might at first lack firmness, their experiences in the two capacities would soon render most of them " as wise as serpents," though " as harmless as doves."

In reforming the medical out-door relief, women would be invaluable Guardians. In dealing with widows, deserted wives, fallen women, and foundlings, it seems hardly necessary to state that the natural person for these offices is a woman and not a man. In almost every branch of the Poor Law work, at all events in all the most important, the advantages are clearly on the side of at least one or two women holding seats on every Board of Guardians. If their presence does nothing else in some places than render the proceedings more orderly, they will not be altogether useless. I am convinced, however, that before long it will be regarded as a matter of course for women to take their place in the administration of the public duty of the Poor Law, an office for which, as I have endeavoured briefly to show, they are eminently fitted.

I would therefore suggest to the new Guardian that not being content with obtaining a seat himself, he should use his best endeavours, at any rate at the second election at which he is a candidate, to promote the return of at least one woman as a colleague at the Board.

CHAPTER XXXIII.

CONFERENCES OF POOR-LAW GUARDIANS.

NE of the most hopeful signs of an improvement in the mode of carrying out the Poor Law, and one of the best means of obtaining a superior class of persons to act as Guardians of the Poor, is the movement now slowly extending of holding periodical conferences of the Chairmen of Boards of Unions extending over a large area, as, for instance, a county or the division of a county. At these conferences usually an officer of the Local Government Board attends, and difficult points in the administration of relief are discussed, experiences are mutually compared, and general policy of action is arranged. Possibly it would make these meetings too crowded, but it would seem desirable gradually to extend them so as to include the Guardians or some of them, say one for each Parish, in addition to the Chairman and Vice-Chairman. This has been done in some cases already, and with benefit, for it must be remembered that the individual Guardians as a rule are those who are most in need of the educational training likely to be gained at these meetings.

The benefits which will follow these conferences can hardly be over estimated. In the first place uniformity in the administration of relief is one of the most obvious consequences, and few points are more important. Without some mutual intercourse it is almost impossible for two Boards of Guardians to act in unison, even though their Unions may be close together. An annual gathering, however, and a discussion on two or three points of common interest on each occasion cannot fail to open the eyes and extend the information of all, and to secure that uniformity of action without which it is impossible to cope with pauperism.

Another obvious advantage is the stimulus which these conferences give to the co-operation between charity and relief. It is unnecessary to dwell here on the importance and advantage of this, as I have attempted to do so in another chapter. They will be found so great that there can be no doubt but that if one Union tried the experiment, it would not be long before, by this mutual comparison of ideas and experiences, the advantages of co-operation with charity would be appreciated, and fully carried out on a general scale in the whole area embraced by the conference.

The education of the children is also another problem which these gatherings would most materially assist in solving. No one can doubt but that the children should be taken out of the Workhouses, and this view has been urged for nearly forty years, and yet 40,000 children remain in the Workhouses to this day (see chapter 26). A conference can mutually agree to supply whatever other system of educational training the leading members, who specially understand the subject, think desirable. They can carry on the experiment over a large area, and with far better chance of success, and at much less cost than any single Union by itself.

As regards the treatment of casuals, very much might be done by these conferences. Casuals so far differ from other paupers (see chapter 16) that any action, however good, of one Board is comparatively useless unless that action is uniform throughout a large tract of country. Not only is a uniform plan necessary, but it must be carried out in the same spirit and with equal firmness in one place as another. These annual meetings might be the means of doing much permanently and materially to reduce the army of casuals roving over the country.

To enumerate all the advantages which might follow from a regular extension of Conferences of Guardians, would be almost to recapitulate most of the points which have been considered in these pages. There would seem to be no reason why they should not, if they became general, promote powerfully the reform of the whole system of relief in those matters in which reform is necessary. The management of the poor is so important that the meeting together of those who have the practical work of administering the law in their hands, in order from time to time to discuss it and to consider amendments for the public benefit, is well worthy the attention of all. The indirect influence of such an organisation in inducing men of position, sound sense, and education, to take upon themselves the office of Guardian must also be remembered as no insignificant indirect result to be expected from these gatherings.

The new Guardian should use his utmost endeavour to secure that, in his own district, such a conference shall form part of the year's programme. He may find it difficult, no doubt, in some places, but if it be impossible to induce his Board to consider the subject, he may gradually secure the same result by working on the members of Parliament, the leading authorities, and the ex-officio Guardians of the district. Some of these at any rate will see the advantages, and will probably consent in the first instance to set the movement on foot in one or two of the Unions of the district. The scheme once commenced will not be long in extending when encouraged in this way.

CHAPTER XXXIV.

FOUNDLINGS.

O incident in the Guardian's experiences is more painful than that relating to the foundlings who are brought into the Workhouse. For an infant, probably only a few days old, to be deserted, and left to be picked up either at the Workhouse gate or somewhere close to the entrance to the House is certainly a most distressing consideration. He, however, will be a fortunate Guardian, or one who lives in a very favoured district if he does not meet with a case or two of this description before he has been long on the Board. The history and the facts connected with many of these little creatures would as they have done both in fiction and actual biography, supply materials for many a thrilling story. Whatever the crime and wrong to which they owe their existence, it must be evident to all that they are themselves deserving of the greatest sympathy, a sympathy however which they rarely obtain. The numbers who are thus annually picked up in England is considerable, being computed to be at least two thousand.

I remember being present just after one of these little children had been found. He was a fine healthy boy of about a month old, and had been discovered under a railway arch close to the station, within a few hundred yards from the Workhouse. No doubt some wretched mother had come down by train and deposited him where he was found, and had then returned again by the next train. I suggested naming him Joseph Arch, but this was not quite approved of. A short time before, at the same Workhouse, an infant girl had been found in a somewhat similar manner. She was named after the parish in which she had been picked up.

Endless other examples might be given of these melancholy cases which occur in all parts of the country, but unfortunately it is not so easy to suggest any course which will directly tend to reduce their number. The establishment of large Foundling Hospitals which is adopted in some countries where the desertion of children is as it were recognised, even if it tends apparently to secure better attention to the infants, no doubt increases the evil of desertion rather than reduces it. In London we have a Foundling Hospital, and some there are who doubt the wisdom of its system, and certainly it cannot be said in any way to tend to reduce the desertion of children.

The Workhouse casual's infants are treated like other permanent inmates of the Workhouse; they are, as I show in another place, often brought up by some of the social failures staying in the Workhouse, and it depends on the accident of the Union in which they find themselves as to what training they obtain.

The usual and, indeed, the only action in such cases

which a Board of Guardians can take is to direct inquiries to be made as to the mother ; but such inquiries of
course almost invariably end in nothing, if, indeed, they
are really attempted at all. The mother cannot be found.
A much more important matter, however, though one of
still greater difficulty, is the finding of the father. It
would be well worth every Guardian's while to spare no
trouble if these cases could be brought home to the father ;
but without, in this respect, laying any blame on the
Guardians, I fear the day is far distant when this will be
practicable.

CHAPTER XXXV.

HE impropriety of any one in the position of a
Guardian acting in any way as a supplier of
goods to the Workhouse, or to the Union
generally, is too evident to require argument.
It is, however, not unfrequently done, if not in a direct
way, yet with very little attempt at concealment, and the
new Guardian will do well not to be too sure that nothing
of the sort takes place under his very eyes. The Act of
Parliament is strict on this subject, and inflicts a heavy fine
on all who infringe its provisions. The wording of the
55 George III. c. 137, s. 6, is as follows :—

" No overseer of the poor or other person in whose
hands the rates, or the providing for, ordering, management,
control, or direction of the poor shall be placed " (4 & 5
William IV. c. 76, s. 51, continues the provisions to
Guardians), " shall either in his own name, or in the name
of any person or persons, provide, furnish, or supply for his
or their own profit any goods, materials, or provisions for

P

the use of any Workhouse, or otherwise for the support
and maintenance of the poor in any such Parish, nor shall
be connected, directly or indirectly, in furnishing or
supplying the same, or in any contract relating thereto,
under pain of forfeiting the sum of £100, with full costs of
suit, to any person who shall sue for the same by action of
debt in any of His Majesty's Courts of Record at Westminster."

I met with a case in my own experience which had, I
believe, been going on for years. The Union used a great
deal of timber ends which were cut up into firewood. On
one particular occasion a large quantity, several hundred
pounds' worth, was purchased just at the end of a Board
meeting, when very few members were present, without
any previous notice having been given. The plea for this
unusual action was that the timber was cheap. The timber
contractor happened to be present by some strange chance.
This became talked about, particularly as the Guardian
who proposed the purchase was engaged carting the wood
from the canal to the Workhouse.

On drawing attention to the Act of Parliament and the
circumstance of a Guardian being a sub-contractor to cart
the timber, which he openly acknowledged he was, the
Clerk of the Board stated, as reported in the local paper,
that "There was a doubt about the matter, and he was not
in a position to say what construction would be put upon
such an act in a court of law." The case was aggravated
by this same Guardian acting on the Finance Committee,
whose duty it was to see to the payments, and also on the
House Committee, whose duty it was to see to the timber
being measured.

In spite of the evident objections to the proceeding the Guardian maintained that he was acting quite correctly, though he undertook not to do it again on the urgent request of several members of the Board ; and, at any rate for a time, this irregular proceeding was put a stop to. One might suppose that most men who held the position of Guardian would at once see the impropriety of such a course of action, but the new Guardian will do well to be on the alert in such matters. The least suspicion of this kind on a Board is sufficient to influence prejudicially its whole action, and cannot be too sharply and quickly put an end to. Every Guardian who really wishes to do what is right will be only too glad to prevent anything of the sort from taking place.

CHAPTER XXXVI.

THE KEEPING OF PIGS IN WORKHOUSE GROUNDS.

 FEW lines must be devoted to this subject, simple and commonplace though it be. The custom of keeping pigs is common in those Workhouses which have a little ground attached to them, and which are sufficiently in the country. Of course there is a good deal of waste from a large institution, even though it be a Poorhouse, and converting it into pork and bacon is not only economical but makes a pleasant occasional change in the officers' diet. If the pigsties be placed right out of the way, no objection can be taken to this arrangement, and no doubt some advantages follow in the Union managing a piggery. Often, however, this precaution is not taken, and the consequences are most objectionable, and even serious. The sties are put for convenience near the buildings, or because, if put farther off, some neighbour at a distance will object, or because the passers-by along the road may draw troublesome attention to the smell. I have seen a row of sties within a very short distance of the Infirmary windows, and absolutely close to the work-sheds used by all the old men for the greater part of the day. The smell was dreadful, and must have been most injurious.

Such an arrangement as this is cruel in the extreme, and the more so because often there is no appeal of any sort whatever. The Guardians form the sanitary authority in many places; and though their inspectors of nuisances may order the removal of pigsties all over the Union, they are hardly likely to complain of their masters and direct them to comply with their own law, if they thus purposely and openly neglect and set it at defiance. The new Guardian should see to this; and if he finds the sties near enough to be at all offensive to any part of the buildings, he should either try and have them removed or else induce the Guardians to give up the piggery altogether.

CHAPTER XXXVII.

INCREASES IN SALARIES AND WAGES.

VERY now and then a general application is made for an increase of remuneration by the officers and servants of the Union. The new Guardian must be prepared for this. In one year I noted that almost every person, except the Master of the Workhouse who, perhaps, deserved it most, came up with the same application, namely, for an increase of pay. We had the chaplain, the doctors of all the parishes, a sort of round robin, in fact, from them; all the relieving officers, the schoolmaster, the schoolmistress, the superintendent of labour, the porter, the night-porter, the superintendent of casuals, and every one else, whether he or she had or had not any claim to consideration. The truth was that in our Union the scale was pitched so low that, even with the increase, everybody was dissatisfied, and only looked forward to sufficient time elapsing when they would be able with decency, and some chance of success, once more to apply for a repetition of the increase.

Nothing is worse for the management of any institution

than for the employés to be in this chronic state of discontent, and the new Guardian, if he find it to be the case,
should look into the matter.   No doubt at times unreasonable claims are made, but as a rule Union officials are not
overpaid.   I have known many excellent relieving officers
drawing less all the year round than not a few of those
who appear regularly before the Board as applicants for
relief whenever they are out of work or ill.   This cannot
be correct, for, as I have dwelt upon in another place, the
duty of a relieving officer requires a man not only of
intelligence and ability, but one also of trust and responsibility, and one whose dress, appearance, and mode of
living should surely place him very much above the paupers
it is his business to relieve.

The periodical consideration of an increase of salary is
of itself a great evil, and it is far better to regulate the
remuneration so that it regularly increases by a self-
adjusting scale.   True, there is some difficulty in this with
relieving officers.   It would not do to pay them so much a
head on the paupers, for that would tend to promote
pauperism, and induce them to bring forward as many
applicants as possible ; nor would it do to reverse the process, and to raise their payment for each pauper less than
a certain maximum, for this might make them hard, and
even induce them to refuse to bring forward cases.   There
seems, however, no reason except that I believe the Local
Government Board does not yet approve of it, why their
salaries should not rise, like a Government clerk's, by a
small increment say of £5 a year, or so much every two
years up to a certain maximum.   This would induce them
to stop at one situation, and prevent the periodical appeal

for increase, and the universal discontent either at its refusal, or at the increase being less than was demanded or expected.

The Master of the Workhouse should certainly be paid on some such scale. I never knew one, however, who was; and, as a rule, his remuneration is very much too low. If he is a good man, and the Master of a Workhouse should always be a good man, he has an enormous power for good or evil in his hands; underpaying him is very unjust, and a great mistake; but if he is at all inclined to go wrong, underpaying him will certainly encourage him in so doing, for he can easily make up his income in an improper manner. He has the means of doing so, and of defrauding the Union to a very great extent, and in a way which it is very difficult, if not impossible, to detect.

Doctors are again even worse paid than relieving officers, but as I stated in the remarks I made on page 48, on medical out-door relief, I trust that this evil will be cured in time. I hope that by the introduction of Provident Dispensaries, doctors will be relieved altogether from the duty of acting under the Unions in out-door cases, or that they will only be required to do so to such a limited extent that there will be no difficulty in making the remuneration sufficient.

The general staff of the Workhouse, be they mechanics or persons in some sort of trust, should all be fairly, if not liberally paid. As piece-work can but be rarely introduced the wages should be quite up to the average of those earned outside, for something must be paid to secure the most steady and the most reliable men. Whenever it can be done a slight increase should be periodically made for long service as a matter of course, and without any appeal being necessary.

The new Guardian will be fortunate in his district if he is not soon troubled with this difficulty. I cannot help thinking that if this be so it will well repay an effort, even though it involve some trouble and the expenditure of much time, to endeavour to get the remuneration of the whole staff on some such permanent self-arranging system as I have pointed out, a system so common in other and larger institutions and services.

CHAPTER XXXVIII.

THE LAW OF SETTLEMENT.

THE question as to which parish a person belongs is often one of some difficulty. If a house is on the border-line, a dispute usually ensues. It has been generally held, that in whichever Union the person lies when asleep, that that shall be regarded as the one to which he belongs. In spite of this rule, quibbles and questions arise which might puzzle the sagest philosopher, and even the most practical man of the world.

An amusing case came before me on one occasion. It appeared that the dividing boundary line, not only cut through the cottage but also through the bedroom. Nay, to make matters worse, it actually divided the bed on which the master of the family was wont to rest at night. It was at last decided that the family belonged to the Union in which the head of this important pauper was pleased to lie, and relief was given accordingly.

I may also give another curious case which came before me. The boundary line here also divided the cottage about in half, the back being in one Union, and the front in another. The relieving officer found the old woman in bed in a back room on the ground floor, which was not within our Union area. On the old man her husband being taxed with this, he stated that he slept in an up-stairs room at the front, and that was in our parish. His wife only slept where she did, because she was too infirm to go upstairs. We allowed them relief from our funds as the clerk ruled that the man was the head of the family, and his sleeping apartment settled the case.

These little difficulties must always occur, for it would be impossible to secure that all property should be alto-gether in one or other Union. The law of settlement, however, in other cases is far from satisfactory. More money is often spent in trying to get rid of a pauper by sending him to a distant Union than that pauper would cost if maintained where he was. Under the present law a person must have lived in a Union one year without ever coming on the rates before he obtains a legal settle-ment in the new Union. Consequently, whenever an applicant for relief is known to have lived a less time than twelve months in the Union, every effort is made to get him passed on to the Union from whence he came, or else to compel that Union to pay the cost of whatever relief may be given from the funds of his newly adopted district. This is especially the case with young girls about to have illegitimate children. The main idea is to get rid of them if possible, and when they apply for ad-mission to the House of the Union where they have been living, they are often sent off to their homes in distant parts of the country. With older persons it is at times difficult to find the legal place of settlement, and the clerk has at times to send some one down to the supposed Union to obtain evidence, and to bring the matter before the magistrates in order to obtain the necessary authority for the removal.

Within my own experience I have known of journeys by the clerk, or one of his staff, being thus made from London to Cornwall, Carlisle, and other equally distant places. All this costs a great deal. True, it may eventually end in one Union getting rid of the burden of some pauper, and saddling him on another district to which no doubt it is strictly right that he should belong. Looking, however, at the question as a national one, it would be far better to consider it in a give-and-take sort of way, and to allow every one was *bonâ fide* living in a Union, however and whenever they may have come there, as at once belonging to that Union. Under any circumstances all Unions get the benefit of those of their poor who leave them and whose history is not traced, and as regards the payment of taxes, there is no delay in imposing them on a new resident. There would seem, then, nowadays to be little reason for maintaining this law of settlement.

I would strongly urge a new Guardian to vote against the expensive investigations which are often proposed in order to ascertain the birth-place or otherwise of some unfortunate pauper, with a view of getting rid of him, and to compel some other Union to pay the cost of his keep.

CHAPTER XXXIX.

THE TREATMENT OF BLIND, DEAF AND DUMB, LAME,
DEFORMED, IDIOTIC, IMBECILE, INSANE, AND OTHER
PERMANENTLY AFFLICTED CLASSES OF THE POOR.

 LARGE field for important and useful work
exists in the providing for the proper management of the permanently afflicted classes. In
the first place the Guardian should certainly
distinguish between cases of permanent and inherited suffering, and others brought about more or less directly or
indirectly by the sufferers themselves. The permanently
afflicted of all sorts embraced in the categories given at the
head of this chapter are not in the strict sense of the word
paupers at all. In the case of the Blind and Deaf and
Dumb, Parliament has expressly provided that relief given
them up to 16 shall not make the parents paupers. Even
if in some of the other cases parents belong to this category, their children who come into the world thus afflicted
require and should receive at the hands of society greater
and not less consideration than children in sound health.
This is so from another and that an economical consider-

ation. If left in their natural condition these children must be useless, if not dangerous members of the community, but if cared for properly and systematically trained it has been distinctly proved that almost all, including the most unpromising idiots, may be improved and even made into useful members of society.

A Guardian should therefore make it his special business to see that no child or young person is being brought up in the Workhouse, or, what is even worse and more common, is allowed by out-door relief to be brought up in his parents' home, unless he is at the same time deriving the benefit of such training as will give him every possible chance of mental improvement and of doing something for a living. The Guardian need not hesitate on the ground of a want of authority, for the Legislature has during the last few years been mindful of these sad cases, and has conferred on Guardians powers which, if they would only use them, would secure to every poor person thus afflicted an efficient training and proper care without the aid of alms at all.

As, however, not a few even of those who really study their duties on the Board are unacquainted with the law, I will shortly abstract the provisions which at present exist for the relief of the permanently afflicted. For convenience I will divide them, firstly, into those relating to provincial and country Unions, and, secondly, into those additional powers, which have been specially given to the metropolis.*

* I am indebted to my esteemed friend Mr. W. M. Wilkinson, The Lawn, Ealing, for much assistance in this chapter. He, as is well known, has made this, as well as all sound measures for the permanent improvement of the Poor, his especial study.

PROVINCIAL AND COUNTRY UNIONS.

(a) *As Regards Children.*

By the 31 & 32 Vict. c. 122 (1868), Guardians of any Union or Parish may, with the consent of the Local Government Board, send any idiotic, imbecile, insane, lame, deformed, deaf and dumb, or blind pauper child to any institution specially treating these cases of suffering. The institution or school thus referred to may be maintained by private subscription, county rate or otherwise, and it is not necessary that they shall have been certified under the Industrial School Act, of 1862, c. 43. The Guardians may pay the full cost to these institutions if the Government Board considers it reasonable, even though that cost be greater, as indeed it must be properly to train these cases, than the average cost of healthy children in the Workhouse.

One difficulty at times may be the obtaining of the consent of the parent. This is essential when the parent or parents are known or in the case of illegitimate children where the mother alone is known. Usually, however, this is more or less in the hands of the Guardians themselves. If consent be withheld, in the case of out-door paupers it is simple, and will usually be effective, to refuse out-door relief to the family till it be granted; in the case of the parent refusing when the whole family are inmates of the Workhouse, though this will be rare, nothing can be done it is true; but in the case of afflicted children brought with a request that they may be taken into the House, and this is no uncommon occurrence, the relief can then be made on the condition only that the person is sent to a proper place of training. Orphans and deserted children under 14 years of age can be sent by the sole authority of the Guardians and the Local Government Board. Those over that age (except of course the idiotic, etc., class) must previously give their consent.

The Guardian will thus see that the powers of the Board are sufficient practically to secure to all indigent afflicted children efficient training in schools or institutions specially adapted to their wants, and that too at the cost of the rates, and without depending on or waiting for the accidental benevolence of the charitable. In spite of this, however, this Act of Parliament is practically a dead letter, the reason being, firstly, that Boards of Guardians know very little about it ; and if they do know about it, they are afraid of the cost of carrying it out ; and, secondly, because indiscriminate charity and the voting system of election, on which most of the existing charitable institutions are founded, render their managers unable and unwilling to take them quietly at the cost of the rates, though the cost be secured to them, and thereby lose the publicity and excitement of a periodically contested election.

(b) *As Regards Adults.*

The Act of 31 & 32 Vict. c. 122, above referred to, applies equally to adults as far as the idiotic, imbecile, and insane are concerned ; not only may they be sent to any institution, but one Board may transfer its idiotic in- mates to another Workhouse, whereby assembling a greater number together, better and more special provision can be made for them. By another Act, that of 30 & 31 Vict. c. 106, sect. 21, Guardians may send and pay for adult blind and deaf and dumb paupers in any hospital or institution established for the reception of persons suffering under such infirmities, and may in addition pay the cost of conveyance to and from the same.

It is therefore obvious that no adult idiotic, imbecile, insane, blind, deaf and dumb persons need be kept like the common paupers in the Workhouse, but that they may all be placed in institutions established for such cases, and paid for by the rates, or be removed to suitable workhouses where the essential special training and comfort can be secured for them. Indeed, were Guardians and charitable persons only acquainted with these matters and willing to act up to them, the whole problem of the management of the afflicted classes would soon be solved. The endless begging on behalf of half-starved institutions might be ended, the voting and canvassing might be abolished,—not only the few favoured who now gain admitance would be benefited, but all. None would have to wait till they were too old to get in, nor be forced in before they were old enough to take advantage of the instruction. As the full payment would be made for all by the rates to which all must contribute, accommodation would be provided for all those who really needed it.

Children and Adults.

All the regulations above referred to apply equally to London, but besides them, the Metropolitan Poor Act of 1867 (30 Vict. c. 6) supplies other and even more extensive provision for the welfare of these poor afflicted classes resident in the Metropolis. Under this Act, not only may Guardians send these cases to institutions, but the Asylum Board, formed from the various Metropolitan Unions, may, at the direction of the Local Government Board, themselves create and maintain the necessary institutions, and the expenses will have to be provided out of the Metropolitan Common Poor Fund, and are thus distributed over the large area of the whole of London. The mode of admission to these asylums is to be laid down by the Local Government Board.

With these powers it is obvious that in London, at least as far as the law is concerned, ample provision exists for the relief, maintenance, training, and proper treatment of all these cases of affliction, and that too without depending on private charity in the slightest degree even for establishing the institutions in the first place.

Having these facts before him, the action of the Guardian should be simple. In all probability he will find many of all ages in the Workhouse of his Union, who are either

idiots, insane, imbecile, blind, deaf and dumb. The children he should use his efforts at once to get sent to some
proper institutions where they may be trained. He would
point out to his brother Guardians, not only the importance of so doing, but dwell on the powers which are given
them by Act of Parliament—powers which it is clear would
never have been conferred were they not intended to be
enforced and made use of. Not content with the children,
though these should certainly have his first thoughts, he
should follow on with the adults, and get them removed
from the Workhouse which is certainly no place for them,
mixed as they so often are with the reckless and the
vicious. They should be sent to some institution where
they may at least be trained to do something for their
living, and be improved mentally as much as possible, by
those powers which they have being developed, so as to make
up as far as may be for the sad privations with which it
has pleased Providence to bring them into the world.

If the Guardian has secured the co-operation of Charity
with the Poor Law in his Union (chap. 29), it will be
comparatively easy to carry out a perfect reform in the
treatment of these afflicted cases. A joint committee of
the Guardians and the agents of Charity and the managers
of the institutions will afford a ready means of at once providing for each case, and with the aid of the grants from
the Guardians every afflicted child could be suitably trained
and every afflicted adult educated as far as it was possible.

The following summary of the laws bearing on this subject will be useful.

Summary of Legislative Powers.

1st.—Guardians have the power to send to Public or Charitable Institutions, and to pay their full cost there, and in the case of Blind and Deaf and Dumb, up to the age of 16, without the Parents becoming Paupers, all poor

4 and 5 Wm. 4th, cap. 76, sec. 56; 25 and 26 Vict., cap. 43, sec. 1, 6, 7, 10; 30 and 31 Vict., cap. 106, sec. 21; 31 and 32 Vict., cap. 122, sec. 42.

$\left\{ \begin{array}{l} (1)\ \text{blind} \\ (2)\ \text{deaf} \\ (3)\ \text{dumb} \end{array} \right\}$ children and adults.

25 and 26 Vict., cap. 43, sec. 1, 10.

$\left\{ \begin{array}{l} (4)\ \text{lame} \\ (5)\ \text{deformed} \end{array} \right\}$ children.

31 and 32 Vict. cap. 122, sec. 13.

$\left\{ \begin{array}{l} (6)\ \text{idiotic} \\ (7)\ \text{imbecile} \\ (8)\ \text{insane} \end{array} \right\}$ children and adults.

2nd.—The Local Government Board has the power to order the Metropolitan Asylum Board, at the cost of the Metropolitan Common Poor Fund, to establish for children and adults, and Guardians may send the Poor to

30 Vict., cap. 6, secs. 5, 15, 21, 22, 61, 69.

$\left\{ \begin{array}{l} (9)\ \text{asylums for the sick,} \\ (10)\ \text{,, \quad ,, \quad insane,} \\ (11)\ \text{,, \quad ,, \quad infirm, and} \\ (12)\ \text{,, \quad ,, \quad other class or classes of the Poor (which includes all the afflicted classes).} \end{array} \right.$

The Local Government Board may direct the Guardians
of a Union or Parish in the Metropolis to provide

30 Vict., cap. 6, sec. 38.　(13) dispensaries.
　　„　　„　sec. 42.　(14) proper places for medical advice.
　　„　　„　sec. 44.　{ (15) medicines and appliances.
　　　　　　　　　　　{ (16) surgical treatment.

3rd.—District Boards (that is, Boards formed by several
Unions), under the same Act, at the direction of the
Local Government Board, may build and maintain out
of the Metropolitan Common Fund, and in the country
out of the Union Funds, District Schools for boarding,
and Guardians may send to such Schools—

30 Vict., cap. 6, sec. 48, 69;
　Poor Law Act, 1844; and 　(17) all poor children
　see 18, 19, Vict., cap. 34, 　(not excluding the afflicted).
　sec. 5.

4th.—The School Board must provide Elementary Education in Day Schools, and may remit fees when poor, and
Guardians may pay the fees, without it being deemed
to be Parochial relief, of (not excluding the afflicted
classes)

33, 34 Vict., cap. 75, sec. 5, 25, 74. | (18) all poor children.

5th.—And may build and keep up new Industrial
Schools, or pay the full cost for all neglected children in
existing

33, 34 Vict., cap. 75, sec. 27, 28. | (19) industrial schools.

6th.—This is in addition to the powers given to Counties
to maintain Industrial Schools under the Act 29, 30 Vict.,

cap. 118, and which are also supported by the Imperial
Exchequer.

7th.—Guardians have the power of boarding out poor
orphan and neglected children under the regulations of the
Local Government Board.

CONCLUSION.

CHAPTER XL.

THE SECOND ELECTION.

T the end of a year, that is, in the following spring, the Guardian's term of office will expire, and his continuing in it will depend not only on himself but also on the will of the ratepayers. He should certainly not retire unless obliged to do so, even though an organised opposition to him as the representative of reform be set up. The position which a Guardian will hold in the estimation of the public and of his brother Guardians at the end of the first year will, of course, be very different to that with which he was selected as a new man. Much will depend on his manner, and the way he has handled the subjects he has brought before the Board. With a section of the ratepayers, that is, with the ignorant, he will be unpopular if they fancy that any measures of reform are likely to lead to an immediate increase of the rates, even though they may ultimately

immensely reduce the cost to the Union. This alone will be
sufficient to lose him their votes. With the educated and
better classes he will be sure of support, though his notions
of relief may offend not a few, particularly of those who
prefer that the haphazard system of alms-giving should
continue.

The most serious form of opposition to him will be that
of his brother Guardians. If they are determined to get
him ejected, it will be a difficult matter for him to retain
his seat, and then only at great personal trouble. His
brother Guardians will, however, rarely resort to this step
unless he has personally offended them, or unless he has in
some way broken into some long cherished personal system,
and thereby disturbed some Parochial jobbery. Usually,
however, when a Guardian, unless his Union is in a *very*
bad state, devotes himself to the work, even though he
may differ from his colleagues, and they may object to him
at first, they will gradually come to respect him, and
even if they do not allow him to carry his reforms, they will
not oppose his re-election.

As I have already stated (chapter 32), it will be well at
the second election to induce a lady to become a candidate,
and also for one or two other gentlemen of position to put
up. In this way the Board may be gradually improved.
Further than this, the old members will before long become
educated, and themselves improved.

In Parochial elections, as possibly in all others, at times
the most extravagant and untrue statements are made.
These contests usually go against the right class of
Guardians, and should, if possible, be avoided. A man
of position, or of education and standing, will not put forth

reckless statements, but his opponents may do so freely. The ignorant will read them, and be induced to vote against the persons so attacked, whereas the educated voters will too often decline to be troubled with the matter and withdraw from both parties. Except, therefore, in Unions where matters are almost hopelessly bad, it is always wiser to avoid an open warfare between the two parties on the Board. At times, it is true, this cannot be done, but usually the calm superiority of one or two Guardians persevering in reforms, and taking advantage of every opportunity from a complete knowledge of the law and its details, will, in the long run, overcome even the obstinacy of ignorance.

If by any misfortune a Guardian, desirous of placing his Union on a proper footing, fails to secure re-election, as indeed may happen, owing to the ignorance of so many ratepayers and the apathy of others, he may console himself with having done his best and with having been ejected from what was at best a thankless office. More than this, he may be assured that his work, even though apparently void of fruit, is not so in reality ; the world does not move very quickly, nor does seed that grows to perfection spring up suddenly. It not the less surely takes root ; and if the rejected Guardian have really sown good seed, it will in time come up, and bring forth fruit in a way that is least expected.

The office of a Guardian of the Poor, by whomever held, as I have already stated, is one of great responsibility. Decisions have often to be arrived at promptly which must influence permanently for good or evil. To be invariably impartial, just, firm, and yet merciful is often no easy matter. Perfection it is true cannot be obtained, but I have ventured to issue these pages in the hope that they may assist in leading to a general and uniform rule of action in each class of case; a rule of action not rigid so as to ignore the differences in human nature, nor theoretic so as to fail in the rough reality of poverty, but firm and practical and based on such principles as shall tend surely if but slowly to the social and moral improvement of even the lowest member of this great community, and lead rapidly to a reduction in the numbers who now swell the ranks of misery, degradation, and pauperism.

For EU product safety concerns, contact us at Calle de José Abascal, 56–1°,
28003 Madrid, Spain or eugpsr@cambridge.org.